The Indian Ideology

By the same author

Passages from Antiquity to Feudalism
Lineages of the Absolutist State

Considerations on Western Marxism
Arguments within English Marxism
In the Tracks of Historical Materialism

English Questions
A Zone of Engagement

The Origins of Postmodernity
Spectrum

The New Old World

THE INDIAN IDEOLOGY

Perry Anderson

VERSO
London • New York

This paperback edition first published by Verso 2013
First published by Three Essays Collective 2012
© Perry Anderson 2012, 2013

1 3 5 7 9 10 8 6 4 2

Verso
UK: 6 Meard Street, London W1F 0EG
US: 20 Jay Street, Suite 1010, Brooklyn, NY 11201
www.versobooks.com

Verso is the imprint of New Left Books

ISBN-13: 978-1-78168-259-3

British Library Cataloguing in Publication Data
A catalogue record for this book is available from the British Library

Library of Congress Cataloging-in-Publication Data

Anderson, Perry.
Indian ideology / Perry Anderson.
   pages cm
Originally published: Gurgaon, India : Three Essays
Collective, 2012.
   Includes index.
   ISBN 978-1-78168-259-3 (pbk.)
1. India–History–Autonomy and independence
movements. 2. India–History–Partition, 1947.
3. India–Politics and government–1947–4. Political
culture–India. 5. Gandhi, Mahatma, 1869-1948.
6. Nehru, Jawaharlal, 1889–1964. I. Title.
DS480.84.A734 2013
954.04–dc23
                          2013019312

Printed in the US by Maple Press

Contents

Foreword   1

1. Independence   7
2. Partition   49
3. Republic   103

Index of Names   183
Index of Authorities   190

Foreword

The origins of this text lie in a book to appear on the emergent inter-state system of the leading powers of the time, covering the United States, China, Russia, India and Brazil – I have written about the European Union elsewhere. Treatment of each of these will be distinct in form, but as in that earlier work on Europe, one state seemed to require more historical background than the others under consideration. In *The New Old World*, that country was Turkey. In the forthcoming volume, it is India. The reasons are in each case the same. Both states are the products of national movements of the early twentieth century, whose history has become the object of official versions of the past, extending pervasively into a present whose shape cannot be adequately grasped without addressing these. Discussion in independent India has never been as constrained as in Turkey. But powerful taboos surround a truthful accounting alike of the ways in which Ottoman and British empires passed away; the *dramatis personae* of their expiry; and the nature of the political orders that succeeded them. This was first brought home to me on registering the reception of Kathryn Tidrick's biography of Gandhi, which appeared in 2007, to which I allude in what follows. Unlike the very different figure of Kemal, writing on Gandhi has never been subject to censorship in India, where critical treatments can be found from the 1920s onwards. Since independence, however, these have been vastly outweighed by a literature of adulation or circumspection. The lack of a single serious notice in the subcontinent of Tidrick's work, the first notable scholarly study of Gandhi's religious and political thinking from his time in England and South Africa to his death, made clear how deep repression of inconvenient historical realities has become, not only in the popular media, but quite widely in the intellectual community of the Union.

Originally appearing, without footnotes, across three issues of the *London Review of Books* in the summer of 2012, an attempt to confront some of these realities is published here, at the initiative of the Three Essays Collective, under a title that alludes to a work of Marx on thinkers of his own country. *The Indian Ideology*, however, deals with another – albeit related – sort of subject: not simply a prevailing set of ideas, but also the conditions and events that generated them, and which they both reflect and distort. The first of these lies in the beliefs and actions of Gandhi, as the central figure of the struggle for independence in the subcontinent, with whom the opening section of the text is essentially concerned. The second involves the way power was transferred from the Raj to Congress after 1945, amid the catastrophe of Partition, whose place in the foundation of the state can be compared to that of the Armenian genocide in Turkey, not in its nature, which was very different, but in a continuing incapacity to come to terms with the disaster. The last concerns the structure of the Indian state as it emerged under Nehru, which forms the focal point of the Indian Ideology of recent years. The record of its first ruler is one question raised, and rarely answered with any degree of candour, by the republic that followed. At a deeper level, what has been the social anchorage of democracy in India, and the bearing of caste on it? What, in turn, is the place of religion in the Union – secular in statement, how far is it in substance? What, finally, are the birth-marks and costs of the unity of the nation?

The Indian Ideology, a nationalist discourse in a time when there is no longer a national liberation struggle against an external power, and oppression where it exists has become internal, obscures or avoids such issues. It is not, of course, the only nationalist ideology of contemporary India. To its right, Hindutva offers a much more aggressive vision of the nation. Nor is it woven simply of myths and delusions. The values to which it appeals, as I make clear, are not mere fictions, and the ideology would be of little effect if they were. But they form so selective a representation of reality that, as a system, they become a discourse that fatally generates a culture of euphemism and embellishment, precluding any clear-eyed stock-taking of past or present. Empirically, few thinkers or writers of any standing offer undiluted cases of it. As a mental framework, it can coexist with a wide range of outlooks that in detail are more critical than or contradictory of it. To reject it is thus not to dismiss the work, often original and substantial, of all those who give expression to the ideology; to do so would make a clean sweep of much, within its limitations or exceeding them, that is intellectually impressive.

The principal carrier of the ideology is the liberal mainstream of Indian intellectual life. There, British influences dating from the Raj have been increasingly replaced by American variants, as the United States becomes the land of consumer reference for the Indian middle class, and of principal academic location for scholars of the diaspora. But it would a mistake to identify the conventional 'idea of India' simply with Indian liberalism, declarative or unspoken. It extends much further, into wide reaches of the area self-defined as to the left of this mainstream. *The Indian Ideology* is a short study, offering a synthesis that in the nature of things has no pretension to exhaustive totalization. Many aspects of the topics it deals with are, by reason of compression, perforce left aside. Other questions remain unaddressed. Of these, the major lacuna is certainly any treatment of the Indian Left. Its fate is absent from these pages. But clearly the sway of the Indian Ideology is also a function of its weakness as a force within society.

The reasons for that weakness have, it would seem, yet to be studied at the depth they demand. The record of Indian communism, from its late birth as a popular movement in the 1930s to its present three-way division, is certainly one replete with errors, strategic and tactical, many imposed by the Soviet party in its heyday, others unforced.[1] But – this I do touch on – the fundamental reason for the relative political weakness of the Indian left, from which those who were socialists could escape no more than those who were communists, lay in the fusion of nation with religion in the struggle for independence. Wherever this occurred – Ireland, where I grew up, is a signal case – the terrain was adverse for the left from the start. In the

---

1 The best retrospect of these, up to the mid-seventies, remains the interview that K. Damodaran gave a year before his death, now republished in Francis Mulhern (ed), *Lives on the Left: A Group Portrait*, London 2012, pp. 67–94, a remarkable testimony to the qualities, human and political, of this admirable revolutionary. For the subsequent thirty-four years of the CPM government in West Bengal, see the critical balance-sheet of Kheya Bag, 'Red Bengal's Rise and Fall', *New Left Review* 70, July-August 2011, pp. 69–98.

subcontinent, that was always, as it has remained, the underlying sociological reality. There is, of course, more that needs to be explained than this. Analytically, the principal puzzle to be solved is why Indian Communism, after initial repression in Telengana, acquired a lasting mass basis only in Kerala and West Bengal, two states of such dissimilar character, and nowhere else in the Union, until the growth of a Naxalite guerrilla, obviously much more restricted, in *adivasi* forest communities. So far as I am aware, no good explanation of this truncated bi-polarity has yet been proposed.

The causes of the marginalization of the Left in Indian politics at large, certainly complex, are one thing. Its consequences for Indian culture are another. Salient among them has too often been a passive accommodation to the myths of the Indian Ideology, and the crimes of the state committed in their name. The hegemony of edulcorated versions of the national past is perhaps the most striking aspect of an internalization of the ruling ideas of the time. If the Left is to gain a stronger place in the intellectual scene, a break with these, in an altogether more confident and critical spirit, is needed. In France, Sartre once famously spoke of *la gauche respectueuse*. In India, the Left has always worked in more difficult conditions, under far greater pressures. But less respect for the pieties of their age was expressed by Ambedkar or Ramaswamy than is accorded those of today by many who conceive of themselves as politically more advanced. The Left would do well to recapture something of their insolence.

1.
Independence

'Astonishing thought: that any culture or civilization should have this continuity for five or six thousand years or more; and not in a static or unchanging sense, for India was changing and progressing all the time', marveled the country's future ruler, a few years before coming to power. There was 'something unique' about the antiquity of the subcontinent, and its 'tremendous impress of oneness', making its inhabitants 'throughout these ages distinctively Indian, with the same national heritage and the same set of moral and mental qualities', he mused. Indeed, a 'dream of unity has occupied the mind of India since the dawn of civilization'.[1]

In patriotic reveries of this kind, today's admirers of Nehru, even some of his critics, are not to be outdone. For Manmohan Singh, his current successor in Delhi, India's struggle for independence has 'no parallel in history', culminating

---

1   Jawaharlal Nehru, *The Discovery of India*, New York 1946, pp. 38, 40, 47, 50.

in a constitution that is 'the boldest statement ever of social democracy'.[2] With no obligation to official bombast, scholars fall over themselves in tributes to their native land. For Meghnad Desai, the 'success story' of modern India in combining unity with diversity is 'nothing short of a miracle'. For Ramachandra Guha, the 'humdrum manifestation of the miracle of India' crinkles in its very banknotes, with Gandhi on one side and their denomination in seventeen languages on the other, its radiance anticipating 'by some fifty years, the European attempt to create a multilingual, multireligious, multiethnic, political and economic community'. For its part, Indian democracy – Pratap Bhanu Mehta declares – is ' a leap of faith for which there was no precedent in human history'. 'Especially fortunate' in its millenial traditions of 'public arguments, with toleration of intellectual heterodoxy', according to Amartya Sen, 'independent India became the first country in the non-Western world to choose a resolutely democratic constitution' – founding an adventure that, in the eyes of Sunil Khilnani, represents 'the third moment in the great democratic experiment launched at the end of the eighteenth century by the American and French revolutions', which 'may well turn out to be the most significant of them all, partly because of its sheer human scale, and partly because of its location, a substantial bridgehead of effervescent liberty on the Asian continent'. This is 'the most interesting country in the world', even the lesser of whose aspects are entitled to their garlands: after independence, its absorption of princely states a 'stupendous achievement', its foreign policy 'a staggering performance'. Nehru himself, 'in the

---

2   Manmohan Singh, 'An Indian Social Democracy: From Political Vision to Practical Possibility', *Indira Gandhi Conference* 19 November 2010, pp. 4, 1. On other occasions, the same ruler has imperturbably apologized to the British for any discomfort caused by the national movement.

hearts and minds of his countrymen' – is 'George Washington, Lincoln, Roosevelt and Eisenhower rolled into one'.[3]

All countries have fond images of themselves, and big countries, inevitably, have bigger heads than others. Striking in this particular cornucopia of claims, however, is the standing of their authors: names among the most distinguished Indian intellectuals of the age. Nor are any of the works from which these tributes come – respectively, *The Rediscovery of India*, *India after Gandhi*, *The Burden of Democracy*, *The Argumentative Indian*, *The Idea of India*, *Makers of Modern India* – either casual or uncritical about their subject. All are eminently serious studies, required for an understanding of the country. What they indicate, however, is something that they share with the rhetoric of the state itself, from Nehru to Singh, the centrality of four tropes in the official and intellectual imaginary of India. Telegraphically, these can be termed the couplets of: antiquity-continuity; diversity-unity; massivity-democracy; multi-confessionality-secularity. Issuing from an independence struggle perceived as without equal in scale or temper, each has in its way become a touchstone of – in a now consecrated phrase – the 'idea of India'. Though by no means every mind of note subscribes to the full bill of particulars, they enjoy what in Rawlsian diction might be called an overlapping consensus. What realities do they correspond to?

3 Respectively: Meghnad Desai, *The Rediscovery of India*, London 2009, p. xii; Ramachandra Guha, 'A Nation Consumed by the State', *Outlook*, 31 January 2011, and *India After Gandhi*, London 2007, pp. 767–768; Pratap Bhanu Mehta, *The Burden of Democracy*, Delhi 2003, p.1; Amartya Sen, *The Argumentative Indian*, London 2005, p. 12; Sunil Khilnani, *The Idea of India*, London 2003, p. 4; Ramachandra Guha, *Makers of Modern India*, Delhi 2010, p. 4; *India After Gandhi*, p. 44; Khilnani, *The Idea of India*, p. 39; Guha, *Makers of Modern India*, p. 8, where the tribute to Nehru comes originally from a Canadian diplomat, but cited without any disavowal, seems fair to take as a judgment of the author *par personne interposée*.

I

For the nationalist movement against the rule of the British, it was an article of faith in the Congress Party that, in Gandhi's words, 'India was one undivided land made by nature', in which 'we were one nation before they came to India' – ancestrally, indeed, 'fired with an idea of nationality unknown in other parts of the world. We Indians are one as no two Englishmen are'.[4] Nehru's claim of an 'impress of oneness', going back six thousand years, persisted from pre-war writings like *The Unity of India* to his final dispute with China, in which the *Mahabharata* could be invoked by his foreign office as proof that the North-East Frontier Agency had been part of Mother India from time immemorial, rather as if the *Niebelunglied* were to clinch German diplomatic claims to Morocco. Such notions have not gone away. The facts gainsay them. The sub-continent as we know it today never formed a single political or cultural unit in pre-modern times. For much the longest stretches of its history, its lands were divided between a varying assortment of middle-sized kingdoms, of different stripes. Of the three larger empires it witnessed, none covered the territory of Nehru's *Discovery of India*. Maurya and Mughal control extended to contemporary Afghanistan, ceased below the Deccan, and never came near Manipur. The area of Gupta control was considerably less. Separated by intervals of five hundred and a thousand years, there was no remembered political or cultural connexion between these orders, or even common religious affiliation: at its height, the first of these Buddhist, the second Hindu, the third Muslim. Beneath a changing mosaic of mostly regional rulers, there was more continuity of social patterns, caste –

---

4   *Hind Swaraj or Indian Home Rule*, 14th reprint, Ahmedabad 2001, pp. 40–41. The book dates from 1909.

the best claimant to a cultural demarcation – attested very early, but no uniformity. The 'idea of India' was a essentially a European, not a local invention, as the name itself makes clear. No such term, or equivalent, as India existed in any indigenous language. A Greek coinage, taken from the Indus river, it was so exogenous to the subcontinent that as late as the 16th century, Europeans could define Indians simply as 'all natives of an unknown country', and so call the inhabitants of the Americas.[5]

When the British arrived, it was the sprawling heterogeneity of the area that allowed them to gain such relatively swift and easy control of it, using one local power or population against the next, in a series of alliances and annexations that ended, over a century after Plassey, with the construction of an empire extending further east and south, if not north-west, than any predecessor. 'India's segmented society and denationalized governments did not constitute a serious challenge to the British', has written one leading native historian: 'Indian troops conquered the country for the British.'[6] There is a touch of exaggeration, and anachronism, in the judgement. But it delivers a basic truth. Foreign conquerors were no novelty in the subcontinent, whose northern plains had known successive waves of them from the tenth century onwards. For many, the British were not necessarily more alien than previous rulers. The latest invaders would, of course, always require their own soldiers too. But if the British could gain and keep a firm grip on such a vast land-mass, it because they could count on its

---

5   Ainslie Embree, *Imagining India: Essays on Indian History*, Delhi-New York 1989, pp. 3, 14–16 ff. The Greeks took their term from earlier Persian reference to the lands beyond the Indus as Hindustan, later often employed by the Mughals.

6   B.B. Misra, *The Unification and Division of India*, Delhi 1990, p. 64.

multiple fragmentations – ethnic, linguistic, dynastic, social, confessional.

For a century after the seizure of Bengal, sepoys in the command of the East India Company outnumbered whites six to one. The Mutiny of 1857, which came as a severe shock, altered the mixture.[7] Thereafter, the policy of the Raj was to hold the ratio at two to one, and make sure that native detachments developed no common identity. Wood, Secretary of State for India under Palmerston, made no bones about the objective: 'I wish to have a different and rival spirit in different regiments, so that Sikh may fire into Hindoo, Goorkha into either, without any scruple in case of need.'[8] Or, as the Eden Commission (1879) would subsequently explain: 'As we cannot do without a large Native army in India, our main object is to make that army safe: and next to the grand-counterpoise of a sufficient European force, comes the counterpoise of Natives against Natives' – for example 'that distinctiveness which is so valuable and which, while it lasts, makes the Muhammedan of one country [note the term] despise, fear or dislike the Muhammedan of another.'[9] The mutineers in Delhi having sought restoration of Mughal power, Muslims were suspect as recruits thereafter, becoming the exception in an Army based on particularist identities – no all-Muslim units were ever allowed within it. The key groups on whom the British came to rely most were, as Wood indicated, Sikhs and Gurkhas, both relatively small communities, joined later by Pathans and Punjabis. Recruits came from among the

---

7   'Mutiny' is, of course, a restrictive term of convenience for what was a much wider rebellion against British rule, by no means confined to the ranks of its sepoys, if one still in the end outweighed by obedience to it.

8   Hira Lal Singh, *Problems and Policies of the British in India, 1885–1898*, London 1963, p. 140.

9   Stephen Cohen, *The Indian Army: Its Contribution to the Development of a Nation*, Delhi 1990, pp. 38–39.

least literate groups in the countryside, with a preference for poor peasants attached to a scrap of land.[10] No natives could become officers, as they could in French colonial armies, until the aftermath of the Great War.

Comprising a peace-time strength of some 200–250,000, the Indian Army was the largest employer in the Raj, and always absorbed a third to a half of its revenue. Regularly deployed overseas, it constituted in Salisbury's famous words, 'a British barrack in the Oriental Seas from which we may draw any number of troops without paying for them'. Its services included provision of soldiers for imperial expansion in the Middle East, Africa and South-East Asia, and cannon-fodder on a heroic scale in the First World War, when 1.3 million mustered for Asquith and Lloyd George. But its primary function remained domestic intimidation, the maintenance of British rule by threat or exercise of force. Laid out across the country, its cantonments were a permanent reminder of what power was master in the land. In the north-west, along the marches with Afghanistan, border fighting and fantasms of Russian invasion kept large forces in the field. But internal security was always the top priority, requiring the use of British troops in greater numbers than native levies, the reverse of deployment on the frontier; Gurkhas – aliens too – assisting as 'praetorians of last resort'.[11] A large police apparatus, already 150,000 regulars by the 1880's, operated as the forward screen of repression. Down to the end, the Raj remained a garrison state, as its Viceroy pointedly reminded the Cabinet in 1942: 'India

---

10 David Omissi, *The Sepoy and the Raj: The Indian Army, 1860–1940*, Basingstoke 1994, pp. 47–50. By 1914 three quarters of all Indian infantry came from the Punjab, the North-West Frontier and Nepal: p. 19.

11 *The Sepoy and the Raj*, p. 209; Christopher Bayly and Tim Harper, *Forgotten Wars: The End of Britain's Asian Empire*, London 2007, p. 406.

and Burma have no natural association with the Empire, from which they are alien by race, history and religion, and for which as such neither of them have any natural affection, and both are in the Empire as conquered countries which had been brought in by force, kept there by our controls, and which hitherto it has suited to remain under our protection'.[12] Attlee, scandalized like any good social-democrat at the utterance of such truths, complained that this was 'an astonishing statement to be made by a Viceroy', sounding like 'an extract from anti-imperialist propaganda speech'.[13]

Coercion, of course, never sufficed on its own: it always required its complement of collaboration. That came from two principal supports. Two-fifths of the territory of the Raj, and a fifth of its population, were left in the hands of princes, mostly Hindu, under the watchful guidance of British residents: feudatories owing the preservation of their wealth and power to the overlord. In the rest of the subcontinent under direct British rule, landlords – Muslim or Hindu – were beneficiaries of the colonial regime, not a few having originally acquired their properties through its good offices, and all enjoying its protection in their exploitation of tenants and labourers beneath them. These forces were natural subordinates of the Raj. Less so were merchants and manufacturers, who came over time to form the nucleus of an industrial bourgeoisie, harmed rather than helped by an imperial economic system designed to give British exports control of Indian markets. Without tariff protection, many came to have as much resentment as loyalty to the

---

12　Linlithgow cable to Amery, in Nicholas Mansergh (ed), *The Transfer of Power*, Vol I, London 1970, § 23, p. 49: 21 January 1942. Henceforward *TOP*.

13　Peter Clarke, *The Cripps Version: The Life of Sir Stafford Cripps, 1889– 1952*, London 2002, p. 278.

Empire. Yet ambivalence was rooted in the conditions of their growth, since it was British railways, binding the subcontinent together geographically, that extended their potential fields of profitable operations, and British rule of law that assured them stable rights of possession and mechanisms of transaction.

Nor, of course, was the modernizing force of the Raj limited to its locomotives and law-books. It was official policy to produce a native elite educated to metropolitan standards, or as Macaulay famously put it, 'a class of persons, Indian in blood and colour, but English in taste, in opinions, in morals, and in intellect'. The confident prescription overlooked the fact that common among such opinions were liberal verities capable of being inconvenient in the Oriental Sea. Two generations later, a layer of articulate professionals – lawyers, journalists, doctors and the like – had emerged, the seedbed of Congress nationalism. The British had taken over the subcontinent with such relative ease because it was politically and socially so tangled and fractured, but in imposing a common infrastructural, juridical and cultural grid on it, they unified it as an administrative and ideological reality for the first time in its history. The idea of India was theirs. But once it took hold as a bureaucratic norm, subjects could turn it against rulers, and the nimbus of empire dissolve into the charisma of nation.[14]

The capsizal was gradual. Congress, founded in the 1880s by a group of lawyers whose leading light was an Englishman, remained for some time a pressure-group of notables seeking

---

14 'We do not encounter in the pre-British past either the idea of an Indian nation or any consciousness of a Hindu community spread across the subcontinent', Tapan Raychaudhuri observes. 'Indian nationalism, the idea that the very diverse population of the subcontinent constituted a nation, was also of course a product of British rule': *Perceptions, Emotions, Sensibilities: Essays on India's Colonial and Post-colonial Experiences*, Oxford 1999, pp. 164–165.

no more than colonial self-government. The first outbreak of more radical nationalist agitation, prompted by Hindu anger at Curzon's division of the province of Bengal, came two decades later. To check it, the Liberal government elected in 1906 introduced a carefully calibrated representative element into the provincial and central legislative machinery of the Raj, allowing for a minority of members in each to be elected on a complex franchise of some 2 per cent of the population. The aim of the Morley-Minto Reforms of 1909 was prophylactic. As Delhi cabled London: 'we anticipate that the aristocratic elements in society and the moderate men, for whom at present there is no place in Indian politics, will range themselves on the side of the Government and will oppose any further shifting of the balance of power and any attempt to democratise Indian institutions'.[15] Congress, while regretting provision for separate Muslim representation, welcomed the changes as a liberal constitutional reform, and expressed its loyalty to the Emperor when George V arrived for the durbar of 1911. Three years later, it gave unstinting support to the Empire in the Great War.

This was the stage onto which Gandhi stepped on his arrival in Bombay in 1914, after twenty-one years in South Africa. Though preceded by his reputation as a fearless spokesman for the Indian community there, he had no experience of political life in the subcontinent, and initially confined himself to study tours and setting up an ashram in Ahmedabad. But by the end of the war, his active support of local struggles by indigo-labourers in Bihar, farmers and textile-workers in Gujarat, bringing tactics he had developed in South Africa to each, had given him a country-wide reputation. Within another two years, he had transformed Indian politics, leading the

---

15 See Judith Brown, *Nehru: A Political Life*, New Haven 2003, p. 43.

first mass movement to rock British power since the Mutiny, and remaking Congress as a popular political force. After the upheaval of 1919–1921, he twice again launched campaigns, in 1930–31 and 1942–43, in size each bigger than the last, challenging the authority of the Raj in successive landmarks of a struggle for national liberation.

In orchestrating these great movements, Gandhi displayed a rare constellation of abilities in a political leader. Charismatic mobilization of popular feeling was certainly foremost among these. In the countryside, adoring crowds treated him as semi-divine. But, however distinctive and spectacular in his case, this is largely a given in any nationalist movement. What set Gandhi apart was its combination with three other skills. He was a first-class organizer and fund-raiser – diligent, efficient, meticulous – who rebuilt Congress from top to bottom, endowing it with a permanent executive at national level, vernacular units at provincial level, local bases at district level, and delegates proportionate to population, not to speak of an ample treasury. At the same time, though temperamentally in many ways an autocrat, politically he did not care about power in itself, and was an excellent mediator between different figures and groups both within Congress and among its variegated social supports. Finally, though no great orator, he was an exceptionally quick and fluent communicator, as the 100 volumes of his articles, books, letters, cables (far exceeding the output of Marx or Lenin, let alone Mao) testify. To these political gifts were added personal qualities of a ready warmth, impish wit and iron will. It is no surprise that so magnetic a force would attract such passionate admiration, at the time and since.

But Gandhi's achievements also came at a huge cost to the cause which he served. The twentieth century saw quite a few leaders of national movements who were men of religion – the Grand Mufti and the Abbé Youlou, Archbishop Makarios and Ayatollah Khomeini, among others. For most, their faith was subordinate to their politics, an instrument or adornment of essentially earthly ends. In a few cases, like that of Khomeini, there was no significant distinction between the two – religious and political goals were one, and there could be no conflict between them. Within this gallery, Gandhi hangs apart. For him alone, religion mattered more than politics, which did not coincide with, but subjoined it. There was a further difference. Not only did he did hold no religious office, but his religion was to a peculiar extent home-made, unlike any existing belief-system at the time. Quite how strange a pot-pourri this was, will not be found in the industry of glozing commentary that has grown up around his ideas, adjusting them for contemporary usage in much the same way as the Pentateuch becomes a blue-print for universalism and the Quran all but a trailer for feminism. We owe the first scrupulous account of it to Kathryn Tidrick's *Gandhi. A Political and Spiritual Life*, which came out five years ago, to a deafening silence, not only in India – that was perhaps to be expected, if not quite the performance of much its best periodical, the *Economic and Political Weekly*, whose scant evasive notice was scarcely even literate[16] – but on the whole in Britain too.

---

16 Diva Dwivedi and Shaj Mohan, 'Gandhi's Life and Thought', *Economic and Political Weekly*, 1–7 January 2011. In a climate where all shades of political opinion in India, from the RSS to the CPM, unite in formal reverence to a national icon, serious critical study of Gandhi is at a discount. The defensive reflexes greeting Joseph Lelyveld's recent *Great Soul* (New York 2011), a deeply respectful, not especially political, biography, that clears some away some of the myths surrounding Gandhi's years in South Africa without greatly questioning his record in India, are representative. In characteristic tones, Rajmohan Gandhi, author of more than one fulsome life of his grandfather, complained – also in the *Economic and*

The composition of Gandhi's faith, Tidrick has shown, was born of a cross between a Jain-inflected Hindu orthodoxy and late Victorian psychomancy, the world of Madame Blavatsky, Theosophy, *planchette* and the Esoteric Christian Union. The two were not unconnected, as garbled ideas from the former – karma, reincarnation, ascetic self-perfection, fusion of the soul with the divine – found occult form in the latter. Little acquainted with the Hindu canon itself in his early years, Gandhi reshaped it through the medium of Western spiritualisms of the period. His one aim in life, he decided, was to attain *moksha* – that state of perfection in which the cycle of rebirth comes to an end, and the soul accedes to ultimate union with God. 'I am striving for the Kingdom of Heaven which is *moksha*', he wrote, 'in this very existence'. The path towards it was 'crucifixion of the flesh', without which it was impossible to 'see God face to face', and become one with Him. But if such perfection could be attained, the divine would walk on earth, for 'there is no point in trying to know the difference between a perfect man and God'. Then there would be no limit to his command of his countrymen: 'When I am a perfect being, I have simply to say the word and the nation will listen'.[17]

Political Weekly (3 December 2011) – that a book 'ignoring every scene of agony, ecstasy, surprise or boldness' could only be a 'bid to belittle Gandhi'.

17 *The Collected Works of Mahatma Gandhi*, Vol 23, p. 349: 3 April 1924 [Vol 27, p. 156]; Vol 55, p. 286: 22 July 1933 [Vol 61, p. 251]; Vol 68, p. 172: 4 December 1938 [Vol 74, p. 276]; Vol 31, p. 69: 29 June 1926 [Vol 35, p. 438]; Vol 27 p. 449: 29 July 1925 [Vol 32, p. 208] Henceforward *CWMG*. The revised electronic version of the Collected Works produced by Indian government in 2000, which integrates material from the supplementary volumes of the original printed edition into a continuous chronological sequence, has been severely criticized by Indian scholars, and officially withdrawn. But since it easier to access, references to it are given in brackets after those to the print edition.

Crucifixion of the flesh, in this conception, meant far more than vegetarian prohibitions prescribed by his caste background. Not in food, but in sex lay the over-riding danger to liberation of the soul. The violence of Gandhi's revulsion against carnal intercourse of any kind mingled Christian fears of sin with Hindu phobias of pollution. Celibacy was not just a duty for the dedicated few. It was enjoined on all who would truly serve their country. 'A man who is unchaste loses stamina, becomes emasculated and cowardly. He whose mind is given over to animal passions is not capable of any great effort'. If a married couple gratified these, it was still 'an animal indulgence' that 'except for perpetuating the race, is strictly prohibited'.[18] At the height of political mobilization, in 1920, even conjugal union was impermissible – all Indians must forego sexual relations, as 'a temporary necessity in the present stage of national evolution'. Complete continence – *brahmacharya* – was of such transcendent importance that an involuntary ejaculation at the age of sixty-five was matter for an anguished public communiqué. At seventy-seven, testing himself by sleeping nude with his great-niece, he wrote: 'even if only one *brahmachari* of my conception comes into being, the world will be redeemed'. If his conception were to be universally adopted, the logical result would be 'not extinction of the human species, but the transference of it to a higher plane'.[19]

---

18 *Hind Swaraj*, p. 73.

19 *CWMG*, Vol 18, p. 346: 13 October 1920 [Vol 21, p 35]; Vol 88, p. 348: 16 July 1947 [Vol 96, p. 60]; Vol 25, p. 252: 21/22 Ocober 1924 [Vol 29, pp. 267–268]. Gandhi tempered his last prescription after Vinobha Bhave persuaded him twelve years later that a couple in need of a child could for the purpose sleep together, if perhaps 'on only one such occasion', but 'apart from this should never engage in the sex act'. Contraception remained a deadly danger, spreading unnatural vice: 'if it somehow or other gains the stamp of respectability, it will be the rage among boys and girls to satisfy their urge among members of their own sex'. *CWMG*, Vol

The extremity of such convictions was not confined to the bedroom. Its evils were age-old. Other, no less deadly dangers were more recent in origin. Gandhi enumerated some of these in the one consolidated statement of his fundamental beliefs, *Hind Swaraj*, written in 1909. There he explained that 'machinery represents a great sin'; that 'railways have spread the bubonic plague' and 'increased the frequency of famines', accentuating 'the evil nature of man'; that 'hospitals are institutions for propagating sin; men take less care of their bodies and immorality increases'; that a peasant needs no 'knowledge of letters', which could only make him 'discontented with his lot', neither 'elementary education or higher education' being 'required for the main thing', to 'make men of us'. All these ruinous innovations were exports of the 'satanic civilization' of the West, whose 'votaries calmly state that their business is not to teach religion' – 'some', incredibly, 'even consider it a superstitious growth'. But 'India will never be godless', and to restore it to its pristine condition, just one effort was required, 'to drive out Western civilization. All else will follow'.[20]

In the years after his arrival in the subcontinent, although he never repudiated them, Gandhi did not insist on such radical atavisms. Sexuality had to be fought, but modernity could be more tactically side-stepped in pursuit of the cause embodied in the title of his work. *Swaraj* was self-rule. Politically speaking, this was in effect a call for Home Rule on Irish lines, though this was not an analogy to which he was ever tempted to appeal, since the national movement in Ireland was identified with two strategies – parliamentary and insurrectionary – both of which he rejected for India. But for Gandhi, self-rule was

---

62, pp. 247, 297 – 6 March, 28 March 1936 [Vol 68, pp. 283, 330].

20 *Hind Swaraj*, pp. 39–40, 51, 76–77, 32–33, 80.

far from simply political. It was mastery of the passions and of the senses in the ascent of the soul to its appointment with divinity. *Swaraj* was a religious imperative, of which its political form was no more than a means to a higher end. It entailed not a struggle to evict the British from India, but a struggle of Indians with themselves that, if won, would bring the British to reason. The method of that struggle was passive resistance – non-violence. Gandhi had come upon this conception in Tolstoy, where it was already suffused with religious yearning. But his own version, *satyagraha* – a neologism he liked to translate as truth-force – was an original development of it. For Tolstoy, unconventionally vegetarian and pacifist as he became in advanced old age, remained a Christian. Gandhi, in drawing on his ideas, gave them a distinctively Hindu cast, fusing them with millenial traditions of a more radical asceticism and extra-terrestrialism. Passive resistance, Tolstoy's term, he felt too weak for the movement he set out to inspire: truth was not passive, it was a force. He had shown how effective it could be in South Africa, where Indians were a small immigrant minority. What could not it achieve on native soil, where they were the totality of the population? *Ramarajya*, he told the crowds at his meetings, was within reach if they followed his teachings – the Golden Age of the god-hero Rama, born in Ayodhya, victor over the demon Ravana, for two thousand years the stuff of Hindu legend.

The original politics of the Congress elite had been studiously secular. Gandhi's take-over of the party not only gave it a popular basis it had never possessed before, but injected a massive dose of religion – mythology, symbology, theology – into the national movement. The power of political mobilization in the register of *Hind Swaraj* was manifest. But it posed an obvious problem. Could the Muslim millions be rallied in the same idiom? In South Africa, Gandhi had been a staunch advocate of Hindu-Muslim unity, and no confessional divisions had marred his campaigns of non-violence there. He himself maintained that all religions preached the same truths, so there was no basis for division. But there the two communities were recent implantations, bound together by a white racism of which they were indifferently victims. In the subcontinent, a long history of conquests and conflicts divided the two.

Nor could Gandhi actually be impartial between the faiths they professed. At a personal level, he was perfectly sincere in holding that all religions were equal before the Lord. At a political level, one religion was, inevitably, more equal than the other. Hinduism was indigenous to the subcontinent, and peculiar to it. Islam was neither. Gandhi came from Gujarat, and his knowledge of subcontinental Muslim culture was very limited. A dutiful son of his faith, he declared 'I yield to none in my reverence for the cow', and warned his son against marrying a Muslim on grounds that it was 'contrary to dharma' and – a telling simile – 'like putting two swords in one sheath'.[21] When he wished in *Hind Swaraj* to explain why India had been one nation long before the arrival of the British, he did not invoke the ecumenicism – alleged or otherwise – of the Emperor Akbar, but 'those far-seeing ancestors of ours who established Shevetbindu Rameshwar in the South, Juggernaut in the South-East, and Hardwar in the North as places of pilgrimage'[22]: holy sites scarcely magnets of national identity for Muslims. No mosques or monuments of Islam feature as pendants. When he announced in 1919 that 'India is fitted for the religious supremacy

21 *CWMG*, Vol 16, p. 320: 1 December 1919 [Vol 19, p 151]; Vol 30, p. 229: 2 April 1926 [Vol 35, p 11].

22 *Hind Swaraj*, p. 41.

of the world', the very claim belying any kind of equality, few could doubt which religion he had in mind.[23] The *Ramayana*, after all, was 'the greatest devotional work in all literature'.[24]

How then was such a Hindu revivalist to unite Muslims in a common national struggle? On the hand, he could not do so on a secular basis without denying everything he believed in. On the other, he was realistic enough to know that reiteration of the precept that all religions converged on the same goal, however frequent and well-meant, might cut little ice with followers of a Prophet who had given famously short shrift to idolatry of the Juggernaut sort. The solution he hit upon was to rouse Muslims to action against the Raj under the banner of Islam itself, in a cause whose overtly confessional objective trumped any of the generic Hindu motifs with which he would colour the national movement. Defeat in the First World War had left the Ottoman Empire at the mercy of the Entente. Its last Sultan before the Young Turk Revolution of 1908, the notorious Abdulhamid II, had sought to prop up a dwindling authority by dusting off his claim to the symbolic title of Caliph, for centuries a worm-eaten relic in the dynastic attic. By 1919 the Allies were in Istanbul. The Young Turks were gone, but – technically, they had never ousted the dynasty – a nominal Sultan remained. What would be the fate of this figure, and the notional pan-islamic authority attached to him?

Under the Raj, Muslims had steadily lost ground after the Mutiny. No longer the masters of the region they had once ruled, not fully trusted as soldiers, they stooped with difficulty to bureaucratic employment by the British, had little business

---

23 *CWMG*, Vol 14, p. 53: 3 November 1917 [Vol 16, p. 116], where he confided that 'the divine word that "India alone is the land of *karma*, the rest is the land of *bhoga* (enjoyment)" is indelibly imprinted on my mind'.

24 *An Autobiography*, Boston 1957, p. 32.

experience, and in possession of an administrative idiom of their own in Persian, did not take readily to education in English. By the turn of the century, it was obvious how far they lagged behind Hindus in government service, industry and the professions. Alarmed at this downward slide in their community, reformers sought to create a better educated Muslim elite, and notables, led by the Agha Khan, prevailed on the British to ensure that Muslim votes would not be swamped by Hindu majorities once a narrow electoral franchise was granted, by allowing them separate electoral rolls and seats. So matters stood in 1914, before taking an unexpected turn with the final denouement of the Great War, the collapse of the Ottoman Empire. In the Arab world, the end of Turkish rule came as a liberation, if a short-lived one, before British and French imperialism divided up the spoils. In the Subcontinent, with no experience of Ottoman oppression, the fall of the Empire was perceived by many Muslims as a humiliation which resonated, emotionally if not practically, with their own descent in the world – the last great Islamic power crushed and dismembered by foes foremost among whom were the British rulers of India. A clamour began that the Caliphate itself was in danger.

For Gandhi, this was an opportunity to demonstrate Hindu-Muslim unity in practice, by rallying Hindu opinion behind agitation to protect the Commander of the Faithful. That more secular Muslims – Jinnah among them – regarded the issue as not merely irrelevant, but thoroughly regressive, a breeding-ground for clerical posturing, did not deter him. Nor was he moved by the dismay of friends who pointed out Arab feelings about Ottoman imperialism, not to speak of the fate of the Armenians. What counted was that this was a religious cause, in which Hindus could join with Muslims against

British injustice. That his fellow Hindus would feel much solidarity over such a strained, remote question was unlikely. But the year 1919, which saw the formation of an All-India Caliphate (Khilafat) Committee, was also the scene of Gandhi's first attempt at an All-India *satyagraha*, protesting the Rowlatt Act that prolonged war-time powers of arbitrary arrest and imprisonment into the peace. Response to Gandhi's call proved patchy, and in the face of harsh repression – including Dyer's notorious mowing down of an unarmed crowd at Amritsar – faded within a few months. But when the official report on this massacre, and the surrounding exercise of martial law in the Punjab, was released a year later – naturally, an extenuation of these – the entire range of political opinion was outraged. In the same month, the draft provisions of the Treaty of Sèvres for winding up the Ottoman Empire were published. The Khilafat campaign had from the outset insisted not only on the preservation of the Caliphate, but its continued guardianship of Mecca and Medina, and control of the Jazirat-ul-Arab, or effectively the whole Middle East. The Treaty did not do away with the dynasty, but severed the Porte from all its possessions in the Arab world. Gandhi promptly denounced it as 'a staggering blow to the Indian Mussulmans'.[25]

Now linking the issues of the Punjab and the Caliphate, while making it clear the Caliphate had priority, in August 1920 he launched a mass campaign of Non-Cooperation with the British. To this he brought all his outstanding gifts of organization, energy and imagination, promising the nation 'Swaraj within a Year'. Non-Cooperation would escalate through four ascending levels of action, if the Raj did not yield: first, renunciation of all titles and honours conferred by the British; next,

---

25 *CWMG*, Vol 17, p. 426: 18 May 1920 [Vol 20, p. 330].

resignation from positions in the civil service; then, resignation from the police and army; finally, refusal to pay taxes. In practice, emphasis fell on boycott of courts, schools, council elections, and – especially – foreign goods. The campaign electrified the country, drawing in social layers and geographical regions hitherto untouched by nationalist agitation, throwing up self-organized volunteer forces for pressure and picketing, setting off stoppages and riots, against the background of the economic hardships of post-war deflation, and a wave of strikes and unionization. Mobilizing Hindus and Muslims alike, and engulfing Calcutta and Bombay in tempests of political unrest, the movement posed the greatest threat to British rule since the Mutiny. Desertions from the civil service, police and army were few, but calls for these were rhetorical gestures by Congress, on which it had not insisted. The ultimate weapon in its arsenal was the last: a tax-strike. The structure of the Raj depended on the land revenue it extracted from an overwhelmingly agrarian population. Without this, it could not be sustained. On 1 February 1922, Gandhi announced that in the face of British obduracy, it was time to proceed to the highest stage of Non-Cooperation. He would initiate refusal to pay taxes in the Bardoli district of Gujarat.

Three days later, police in the small town of Chauri Chaura in UP fired on a crowd protesting food prices, killing three demonstrators; counter-attacking, the infuriated crowd put paid to the policemen in the station where they had barricaded themselves. On learning the news of this unthinkable event, Gandhi declared a five-day fast of penance, and to general stupefaction, without consulting anyone, called off the whole national movement. He could do this, because such was by this time his aura that Congress had granted him 'sole executive power' – in effect, dictatorial powers – six weeks earlier. No single decision of his would ever be as fateful as this. How did he justify it? He had sinned, he explained, in failing to realize that the Indian masses were not yet spiritually advanced enough to adhere to the non-violence which he had always said was a condition of obtaining Swaraj within a year, as he had promised.

It is conventional to take this explanation at face-value. Certainly Gandhi had shown increasing unease at the turbulence his campaign had unleashed in India, the incident occasioning his volte-face perhaps only a final straw. Yet, contrary to legend, his attitude to violence had always been – and would remain – contingent and ambivalent. At the start of his career, as is fairly well known, he twice volunteered for active service, albeit stretcher-bearing, for British colonialism in South Africa – first in the Boer War, and then in the crushing of the Zulu rebellion of 1906. These engagements preceded his exposition of *satyagraha* in *Hind Swaraj*, and could be taken as the stumblings of a pre-Damascene. But when the First World War broke out, he was not only still eager to organize an ambulance corps for the British war effort in 1914, but in mid 1918 went out of his way to try and drum up recruits for the inter-imperialist slaughter in Flanders, tramping as far as Bihar in a bid – happily a dismal failure – to round up more villagers for the trenches. 'The ability to use physical force is necessary for a true appreciation of *satygraha*', he told them. 'He alone can practise *ahimsa* who knows how to kill' – in fact, 'practise of *ahimsa* may even necessitate killing'. Reassuring wives that if they lost husbands 'console yourselves with the thought that they have fallen in the discharge of their duty and they will be yours in your next incarnation', he urged his listeners to 'fight unconditionally unto death with the Briton'.[26]

---

26 *CWMG*, Vol 14, pp. 454, 485, 489 26 June, 17 July, 18 July 1918 [Vol 17,

Did he then change his mind in planning the strategy of Non-Cooperation in 1920? On the eve of the campaign, he had expressly allowed for *bavures* in the struggle. Great movements could not be halted if a people went astray. 'No general worth the name gives up the battle, because he has suffered reverses, or which is the same thing, made mistakes'. Indeed, so far flinching at the prospect of hitches, he declared: 'I would risk violence a thousand times [rather] than risk the emasculation of a whole race'.[27] Nor was the remorse at Bardoli in any way conclusive. Twenty years later, he would tell compatriots: 'We have to take the risk of violence to shake off the great calamity of slavery'. Indeed, 'supposing a non-violent struggle has been started at my behest and later on there is an outbreak of violence, I will put up with that too, because it is God who is inspiring me and things will shape as He wills. If He wants to destroy the world through violence using me as his instrument, how can I prevent it?'.[28] In 1942 he told reporters that in India 'rivers of blood' might be 'the price of freedom'. In 1946, thumping the table, he told the Viceroy 'If India wants blood, she shall have it'.[29]

Such is the record. To read it as evidence of mere hypocrisy on Gandhi's part would be a mistake. There can be no doubt that he was, so far as he himself went, sincere enough in his commitment to non-violence. But as a political leader, his conception of himself as a vessel of divine intention allowed him to escape the trammels of human logic or coherence. Truth was not an objective value – correspondence to reality, or even (in

pp. 101, 131, 135].

27 *CWMG*, Vol 18, pp. 92, 117: 28 July, 4 August 1920 [Vol 21, pp. 93, 117].

28 *CWMG*, Vol 76, pp. 160, 334: 28 May, 26 July 1942 [Vol 82, p. 338; Vol 83, p. 139].

29 *Wavell: The Viceroy's Journal* (ed Moon), Oxford 1973, p. 341.

a weaker version) common agreement – but simply what he subjectively felt at any given time. 'It has been my experience', he wrote, 'that I am always true from my point of view'. His autobiography was subtitled *The Story of My Experiments with Truth*, as if truth were material for alteration in a laboratory, or plaything of a séance. In his 'readiness to obey the call of Truth, my God, from moment to moment', he was freed from any requirement of consistency. 'My aim is not to be consistent with my previous statements', he declared, but 'with truth as it may present itself to me at a given moment' – indeed, 'since I am called "Great Soul" I might as well endorse Emerson's saying that "foolish consistency is the hobgoblin of little minds".'[30] The result was a license to say whatever he wanted, regardless of what he had said before, whenever he saw fit.

The effects of such a conviction on the political culture of the movement that he led could not but be corrupting. Admirers point out that Gandhi nearly always replied, calmly and courteously, often with a touch of wit, to anyone who wrote to him, high or low. He was an impeccable correspondent. But to real intellectual exchange he was a stranger. He was trained as a British barrister, and argued like one, as a lawyer not a thinker, changing his brief from day to day. Not fees, but faith was the condition of this ductility. His religious belief in himself was rock-like, impervious to doubt or objection, guaranteeing in the final resort that all he said, no matter how apparently contradictory, formed a single bloc of truth, as so many scattered words of God. For while he modified or diluted or inverted positions as time went by, enabling a vast

---

30 *CWMG*, Vol 55, p. 61: 29 April 1933 [Vol 61, p.24]; *CWMG*, Vol 42, p. 469: 13 February 1930 [Vol 48, p. 314]. 'In my opinion there is a consistency running through my seeming inconsistencies, as in nature there is a unity running through seeming diversity'.

industry of later glossators to represent him as transcending earlier limitations in a spiritual progress towards ever greater political wisdom, he scarecely ever directly disavowed anything significant he had once said or written. Even his ardour for the wars of British imperialism, for which he was reproached by those who had opposed them, elicited no regret – he had acted in a sincere belief of the honourable intentions of the Empire, and it was not his fault if it had failed to live up to them. *Hind Swaraj*, its battery of archaisms a stumbling-block to those who pointed out he was using railways and doctors and not actually rejecting schools, he defended to the end, writing in 1945 that he still stood by its system of government. Characteristically, he added: 'It is not necessary for me to prove the rightness of what I said then. It is essential only to know what I feel today'.[31] Throughout his career in India, he claimed both to rise above consistency – growing 'from truth to truth', it was to his latest version the world should attend – and unswervingly to embody it. 'Whenever I have been obliged to compare my writing even of fifty years ago with the latest, I have discovered no inconsistency between the two'.[32]

Thus at the crux of 1922, when Gandhi called off the mass movement he had launched, his dismay at a local breach of non-violence was genuine enough, but insufficient to determine his decision – he would take exactly the opposite line in 1942, envisaging such outbreaks in advance. The efficient reason for his sudden retreat lay less in his religious beliefs, whose very fixity allowed for such flexibility, than in his political outlook, connected as the two ultimately were. The goal of Non-Cooperation was *Swaraj* within a year. What did that mean? In

31   Nehru, *A Bunch of Old Letters*, London 1958, p. 506.
32   *CWMG*, Vol 70, p. 203: 30 September 1939 [Vol 76, p 356].

January, a month before his decision at Bardoli, Gandhi spelt out what it did not mean: 'Assuming that Great Britain alters her attitude as I know she will when India is strong, it will be religiously unlawful for us to insist on independence. For it would be vindictive and petulant'.[33] What India should seek was a status like that of South Africa, within a commonwealth of equal partners that retained the British connexion. Six years later he repeated his opposition to any demand for independence, a notion unintelligible to the masses, as opposed to *swaraj* – 'it would be sacrilege to displace that word by a foreign importation of doubtful value'. Making clear the difference was not merely terminological, he declared: 'My ambition is much higher than independence'. To head off pressures for it from a younger generation in Congress, he invoked a loftier national eminence to come: a 'world commonwealth', in which India would no longer be an equal but 'the predominant partner, by reason of population, geography and cultural antiquity'.[34]

Gandhi's resistance to calls for independence stemmed from the same fear that governed the abrupt quietus he delivered to Non-Cooperation. He did not want to evict the British in India if to do so was to risk a social upheaval. Revolution was a greater danger than the Raj. Behind his refusal of any prospect of it lay both religious belief and social calculation. On the one hand, Hinduism bound all who adhered to it into a single interwoven community, in which each was allotted their appointed station. To break its unity by setting one part against another was contrary to divine order. On the other hand, the movement he called into being in 1919 was extensive, but not comprehensive. The Congress he commanded was a coalition

---

33   *CWMG*, Vol 22, p. 140: 5 January 1922 [Vol 25, p. 389].
34   *CWMG* Vol 35, pp. 456–457: 12 January 1928 [Vol 41, pp. 105–106].

with determinate frontiers. It comprised industrialists, traders, professionals, and better-off peasants; it did not include urban workers or the rural poor who formed the vast majority of the population. To pit these against their employers or landlords was to divide what God had joined; to mobilize them against their rulers, to risk setting fire to the country. Class conflict was out. 'We must gain control over all the unruly and disturbing elements', Gandhi explained as labour unrest boiled up during Non-Cooperation. 'In India we want no political strikes'.[35] In the countryside, he 'deprecated all attempts to create discord between landlords and tenants and advised tenants to suffer rather than fight', in the cause of preserving national unity.[36] Property was a trust that had to be respected, and – should that be necessary – protected. Under the Raj, such protection was afforded by the law and its guardian, the police. In Chauri Chaura, a mob propelled by economic grievances had respected neither, in an awful warning of what popular passions might unleash in India. At all costs, their momentum had to be stopped.

Bardoli, where Gandhi had planned to lead a refusal of the land revenue, was an area within his native Gujarat where Congress was well implanted and he knew at first hand. It was also, however, within the zone of *ryotwari* cultivation, where peasants paid taxes directly to the state, rather than in the huge *zamindari* sector where taxes were collected in the form of rent by landlords, passing on a due proportion to the state, and refusal of the revenue would mean a social revolt against them. But even in its most cautious form, a tax-strike threatened the existence of the Raj, by pulling out its economic infrastructure

---

35 *CWMG*, Vol 20, p. 228: 15 June 1921 [Vol 23, p. 285].

36 *CWMG*, Vol 19, p. 352: 13 February 1921 [Vol 22, p. 337].

from under it, and therewith its ability to enforce its will coer-
cively. If it were observed country-wide, imperial law and order
would face, not a nebulous *swaraj* within a year, but a complete break-down.[37] This was the spectre – as he saw it, Chauri
Chaura writ large – at which Gandhi drew back. The Raj must
get its revenue if it was, as he wished, to remain on Indian soil.

While this drama was unfolding in India, a battle in parallel was being fought in Ireland. By the summer of 1920,
Non-Cooperation and the War for Independence were in progress together. Gandhi called off the first in February 1922, as
British forces were sent packing by the second – the Treaty
conceding the Irish a Free State had been signed just two
months before, and by May the twenty-six counties were shot
of them. Since the mid-nineteenth century, Britain had always
stationed a much higher number of troops relative to population in Ireland than in India, with a lower proportion of local
recruits: typically, a military establishment of about 25,000,
and a constabulary of 10,000, for an island of four and half
million inhabitants, less than a hundred miles from England –
a ratio of 1: 130. In India, four thousand miles away, where the
machinery of repression mustered some 400,000 for a population of three hundred million, the comparable figure was 1:750.
Yet within less than three years, an Irish guerrilla force of not
more than 3,000 combatants at any one time had destroyed the

---

37 'Gandhi had been terrified by the prospect of finding India "liberated"
overnight, without either the British army or police to assist Congress in
maintaining order', Stanley Wolpert notes. He may also have been thinking ahead. 'Many of Gandhi's more radical followers later urged him to
call upon all of India's peasantry to stop paying land revenue for a single
year as the fastest way to immobilize British rule, but he recognized the
potential danger that popularizing so revolutionary a technique might
pose to any nationalist successor government': *A New History of India*,
New York 2000, pp. 307, 296.

colonial police and effectively driven the colonial army – upped
to 40,000 for counter-insurgency – from the field in the larger
part of the country. Had there been any synchronized campaign
in India, with its hugely more favourable balance of potential
forces, not to speak of logistics, the issue could hardly have been
in doubt. Instead, there was the fiasco of Bardoli, and the post-
ponement of independence for a quarter of a century. The price
of national liberation was not small in Ireland: division of the
country, and civil war. But it was tiny compared with the bill
that would eventually be paid in India.

Its first installment came when Non-Cooperation was
scuttled. Muslims, once stirred to action and then unceremoniously abandoned by Gandhi, by and large never trusted him
again. Jinnah, a member of Congress long before Gandhi, and
architect of its Pact with the Muslim League (of which he was
by then simultaneously President) at Lucknow in 1916, had
already left the party in a mixture of dismay at the radicaliza-
tion of its tactics, and disgust at the sacralization of its appeals,
once Gandhi took over. Disliking intensely what he saw as the
confessional demagogy of the Caliphate campaign, when it col-
lapsed he sought a second arrangement between the League
and Congress for constitutional advance within the electoral
machinery of the Raj, expanded since 1920 to give a vote to
6 per cent of adult males and more leeway at central and provincial level to the native elite. In 1927, he proposed a pact that
would reserve Muslims one-third of the seats in a central legislature in exchange for a single rather than separate electorates.
Nehru *père*, charged with drawing up its constitutional proposals by Congress, at first accepted this. Then he produced a
Report reducing the quota to a quarter, and rejecting any reservations in Punjab and Bengal, where Muslims were a majority

of the population but a minority of the electorate – elsewhere, he remarked, they could be 'settled by throwing them a few crumbs here and there'.[38] At an All-Party Conference in Calcutta, Jinnah's attempt at amendments were shouted down. A penultimate chance of unity between the two communities was cast to the winds.

By 1928 Gandhi, after a spell in the wings, was front-stage again, and Congress membership increasing by leaps and bounds, a recruitment drive lifting it from 80,000 to 450,000 by 1929. Faced with resurgent nationalist mobilization, the incumbent Viceroy, the future Lord Halifax, promised India what Gandhi had by now redefined as the Swaraj he sought, Dominion status within the Empire. When talks failed to extract fine print from the pledge, Gandhi unleashed his second great campaign in March 1930, of Civil Disobedience, whose spectacular first act was a march to the sea in defiance of the state's salt tax, which had recently been increased. This time, the response was geographically wider, but communally narrower – virtually no Muslims took part – and the repression swifter and greater: sixty thousand arrests, including the entire top leadership of Congres, double the number in Non-Cooperation. But salt was not land, the danger to the Raj far less. In practice, the tax mostly continued to be collected and little revenue was lost, the main impact of the movement coming once again from mass boycott of foreign goods. Unrest was sufficient, however, for the Viceroy to release Gandhi and reach a deal with him to suspend the movement and attend the Round Table Conference on constitutional reform in London, assembling dignitaries from zones of both direct and indirect rule in India, which Congress had hitherto boycotted.

---

38 Mushirul Hasan, *Nationalism and Communalism,* Delhi 1991, p. 279.

At the Conference, Gandhi – unaccustomed to multilateral negotiation – was baulked by Muslim and Sikh insistence on separate electorates, and disconcerted by demand for the same from the Untouchable leader Ambedkar, within what he saw as his own community. Returning empty-handed to India, he resumed Civil Disobedience. A tougher British crack-down saw him jailed again, with further mass arrests, and by the spring of 1932, the movement had been defeated, with nothing tangible to show for it. In the summer, London announced that Untouchables would be granted separate electorates. Caste was now, irrevocably, on the table, and for the first time, Gandhi's religious beliefs were put to a direct political test. What was his attitude to caste ? He had set it out while Non-Cooperation was surging, in 1920–21. Untouchability was a heinous crime. But it was an excrescence that had nothing to do with caste itself, which was 'not a human invention, but an immutable law of nature itself'.[39] There was no element of hierarchy in it. 'The caste system is not based on inequality, there is no question of inferiority', for 'if Hindus believe, as they must in reincarnation, transmigration, they must know that nature will, without any possible mistake, adjust the balance by degrading a Brahmin, if he misbehaves himself, by reincarnating him in a lower division, and translating one who lives the life of a Brahmin in his present incarnation to a Brahminhood in his next'. There was no need to adjust the balance in this life: 'interdrinking, interdining, intermarrying, I hold, are not essential for the promotion of the spirit of democracy'.[40]

---

39 See André Béteille, *The Idea of Natural Inequality and Other Essays,* Delhi 1987, p. 19.

40 *CWMG*, Vol 19, pp. 84–85: 'I believe the caste system has saved Hinduism from disintegration'.: 8 December 1920 [Vol 22, pp. 66–68].

On religious grounds, it was essential to preserve the division of society into four fundamental castes, for it was this which had saved Hinduism from disintegration. 'If Hindu society has been able to stand it is because it is founded on the caste system. The seeds of *Swaraj* are to be found in the caste system'. To destroy it would mean that 'Hindus must give up the principle of hereditary occupation which is the soul of the caste system. The hereditary principle is an eternal principle. To change it is to create disorder. I have no use for a Brahmin if I cannot call him a Brahmin throughout my life. It will be chaos if every day a Brahmin is to be changed into a Shudra and a Shudra is to be changed into a Brahmin'.[41] Caste, indeed, was not just the cornerstone of Hindu India. Properly respected, it might be a universal balm: 'it can be offered to the world as a leaven and as the best remedy against heartless competition and social disintegration born of avarice and greed'.[42]

Over time, he would tone down such claims. Trying to fend off Ambedkar's attacks, he would later explain that the fourfold order of *varna* was not to be confused with sub-divisions of *jati*, which were a deplorable corruption of it, disavowing the latter – 'caste has nothing to do with religion. It is a custom whose origin I do not know and do not need to know for the satisfaction of my spiritual hunger', while continuing to uphold the former – '*varna* and *ashrama* are institutions which have nothing to do with castes. The law of *varna* teaches us that we have each one of us to earn by our bread by following the ancestral calling'.[43] In due course, he would try to dilute *varna* itself

41   See B.R. Ambedkar, *Gandhi and Gandhism*, Jullundur 1970, pp. 128–129.

42   'Caste vs Class', *Young India*, 5 January 1921, p. 2: omitted from *CWMG*.

43   *CWMG*, Vol 63, p. 153: 18 July 1936 [Vol 69, p. 226]. Historically and politically, this was a distinction without a difference, as might be deduced from the know-nothing clause accompanying it, followed by: 'I

with successive adjustments to make it more palatable to egalitarian opinion, at the cost of emptying it of any content save the irreducible core of its identification wth Hinduism itself, as religious belief in the moral duty of hereditary avocation and its bearing on the transmigration of the soul.[44] These he never abandoned.

The threat to Gandhi posed by the prospect of Untouchables gaining the right to their own electorates thus went much

---

am aware that my interpretation of Hinduism will be disputed by many besides Dr Ambedkar. That does affect my position. It is an interpretation by which I have lived for nearly half a century and according to which I have endeavoured to the best of my ability to regulate my life' – as if personal conduct were of any relevance to the structure of a social institution.

44 In a first, tentative phase, perhaps all but a very few Hindus should become Vaishyas like himself: *CWMG*, Vol 35, p. 253 – 17 November 1927 [Vol 40, p. 387]; in a second, more assertive phase, every Indian be a Shudra: *CWMG*, Vol 51, p. 350 – November 5 1932 [Vol 57, p. 335]; in a third, increasingly desperate, phase, all regard themselves as Harijans: *CWMG*, Vol 82, p. 86 – November 16 1946. Obviously, such contortions made nonsense of the ideal of varna itself. But to have repudiated it altogether would have been to shed Hinduism, a step unthinkable for Gandhi, who in all sincerity adjusted his pronouncements to the requirements of the time, but not to the point of rejecting his faith. The final stage of his career, represented by apologists as transcending earlier limitations, also saw the climax of his supernatural beliefs. In his last eighteen months, he told the world that mumbling incantations to Rama was an 'infallible remedy' against illness of any kind. 'My claim is that the recitation of Ramanama is a sovereign remedy for our physical ailments'. Indeed, 'the more I think about it, the more convinced I am that Ramanama, recited from the heart and with full realization, is the panacea for all our ills', so 'if India could realize the power of that principle, not only would we be free but we would be a land of healthy individuals too – not the land of epidemics and ill-health we are today'. For 'when Ramanama holds sway, all illness vanishes. People have no idea of the potency of Ramanama. I am out to demonstrate it. I must wish to live only to serve Him and live, therefore, through His Grace alone': *CWMG*, Vol 83, pp. 234, 263, 413 – 10 March, 22 March, 7 April 1946; Vol 89, p. 273 – 2 October 1947 [*CWMG*, Vol 90, pp. 58, 88, 246; Vol 97, p. 26].

deeper than fear of another British device to divide the national movement, like the separate rolls granted to Muslims, real though this was. More fundamental questions were at issue. If Untouchables were to be treated as external to the Hindu community, it would be confirmation that caste was indeed, as its critics had always maintained, a vile system of discrimination, relegating the lowest orders of society to a subhuman existence with which the smallest brush was pollution, and since Hinduism was founded on caste, it would stand condemned with it. To reclaim the Untouchables for Hinduism was thus an ideological imperative for the reputation of the religion itself. But it was also politically vital, since if they were subtracted from the Hindu bloc in India, its predominance over the Muslim community would be weakened. There were 'mathematical' considerations to bear in mind, as Gandhi's secretary delicately reported his leader's thinking on the matter. Most menacing of all, Gandhi confided to a colleague, might not Untouchables, accorded separate identity, then gang up with 'Muslim hooligans and kill caste Hindus?'[45]

To cut off these dangers, Gandhi – still in prison – announced that as 'a man of religion' and leader of 'numberless men and women who have childlike faith in my wisdom',[46] he would fast to death until the award was rescinded and Untouchables were bundled back into the Hindu electorate. The sensation was enormous. Ambedkar was summoned post-haste to his jail in Poona to avert the passing of the Great Soul. His own view of the religion he was being told to embrace was unflinching: 'No matter what Hindus say, Hinduism is a menace to liberty, equality and fraternity' – words few Indian

---

45 Pyarelal, *The Epic Fast*, Ahmedabad 1932, p. 6; *The Diary of Mahadev Desai*, Vol I, Ahmedabad 1953, p. 301.

46 Pyarelal, *The Epic Fast*, p. 12.

intellectuals would dare utter today.[47] Gandhi, though he had long condemned Untouchability as odious, had never taken any drastic political action against it: sin it might be, but not sufficiently mortal to warrant a fast unto death. Granting Untouchables their own rolls was another matter: against that he would put his life on the line. Under colossal public pressure, and physical threats to him and his community if he stood firm, Ambedkar yielded to Gandhi's blackmail.

A 'Pact' was reached to give a larger number of reserved seats to Untouchables elected, not by their own kind, but by Hindus at large – depriving the community of political autonomy by ensuring that Congress could pick its Uncle Toms for these places. In 1918, after he had fasted to secure a settlement of a wage dispute in Ahmedabad, Gandhi had expressed some misgivings, telling his *ashram* after the event: 'My weak condition left the mill-owners no freedom. It is against the principles of justice to get anything in writing from a person or make him agree to any conditions or obtain anything whatever under duress. A *satyagrahi* will never do so'.[48] Employers were entitled to such scruples. Untouchables would be beneficiaries of a higher consistency. Of the *satyagraha* of 1932, Ambedkar wrote: 'there was nothing noble in the fast. It was a foul and filthy act. The fast was not for the benefit of the Untouchables. It was against them and was the worst form of coercion against a helpless people', forcing them 'to agree to live on the mercy of the Hindus'.[49] He regretted his capitulation at Poona to the last.

47 *Pakistan or the Partition of India*, Bombay 1946, p. 354.

48 *CWMG*, Vol 14, pp. 265–266: 18 March 1918 [Vol 16, p. 344].

49 *Gandhi and Gandhism*, p. 72. A year later Gandhi, admitting that his performance at Poona 'did unfortunately coerce some people into action which they would not have endorsed without my fast', explained that this 'did not cut to the root' of the matter, since 'in any examination of moral conduct, the intention is the chief ingredient', and 'one may not be

Victory over Ambedkar could not alter checkmate by the Raj. For another two years, after civil disobedience had been crippled as collective action, Gandhi persisted with 'individual' acts of it, in and out of fasts and prisons, touring and preaching against untouchability, to purify the religion that had invented it. Eventually, in the spring of 1934 he allowed Congress to call off the liability of its formal commitment to a campaign now defunct. The government lifted its ban on Congress, and a few months later he announced his resignation from the party. The gesture did not mean he was retiring from politics. He was withdrawing to a position from which he could dictate policy when he wished, without having to take responsibility for day-to-day decisions of Congress where he was not in sympathy with them. He could rely on the incumbent President of the party, a conservative Bihari associate, and his successor, the younger Nehru, not to challenge his authority if he chose to exercise it.

By the end of the decade, however, a new cohort was starting to do so, pressing both for Congress to adopt socialism as a goal, and more radical measures to dispatch the Raj. Gandhi had always rejected any talk of socialism, as a breach of the sacred trust in which capitalist property was legitimately held, threatening to have nothing to do with the party if it took it up. The leader of the new left-wing current, Subhas Chandra Bose,

---

deflected from the right course for fear of unintended consequences'. His intention had been only to 'influence both the caste and Harijan Hindus', and 'most decidedly not to induce, irrespective of merits, the decision I desired' (*sic*). To his satisfaction, 'the intention was completely fulfilled and to that extent the fast was not, therefore, from a practical standpoint, open to objection. That it went beyond the intention and coerced some people into giving a decision against their conviction was unfortunate. But such conduct is of daily occurrence in the ordinary affairs of life': *CWMG*, Vol 55, pp. 410–411 - 9 September 1933 [Vol 61, pp. 376–377]. There could scarcely be a purer illustration of Gandhian ethics.

a Bengali heading the Congress Youth Orgnization, also stood for a coalition with the Muslim peasant party in his native province, no less anathema to the Marwari businessmen of Calcutta, Hindu chauvinists to a man, than his socialism. The wealthiest of these, the magnate G.M. Birla, not only bank-rolled Congress to the tune of millions of rupees, but was a long-time follower and intimate of Gandhi, 'dazzled' by his 'superhuman personality'.[50] When Birla made his feelings known, Gandhi put his foot down, and the Congress High Command duly scuppered Bose's inter-communal initiative. Soon after Bose, whose combination of fearless militancy and commanding intellectual gifts had made him hugely popular in the party, was nonetheless elected president of Congress. In the following year he was re-elected, defeating Gandhi's candidate in the first contested election for the presidency in the party's history. This was an unprecedented affront, which Gandhi, who was not prepared to let democracy get in the way of his will, swiftly punished, toppling Bose in an inner-party coup, and then forcing him out of Congress altogether.[51] In the late thirties, his sporadic interventions more often blocking than taking initiatives, such was more or less the sum of his achievements.

When the Second World War broke out, however, he took centre stage again for the last time. With limited knowledge of, or interest in, the outside world – admiring Hitler as, in his way, a fellow-ascetic, since ' He has no vices. He has not married. His character is said to be clean'; ' although he works all his

---

50 Judith Brown, *Gandhi and Civil Disobedience: The Mahatma in Indian Politics, 1928–34*, Cambridge 1989, p. 384.

51 For these events, see Sugata Bose, *His Majesty's Opponent: Subhas Chandra Bose and India's Struggle Against Empire*, Cambridge MA 2011, pp. 150–164, a biography by a descendant in which ancestral loyalty has not overpowered intellectual balance and sobriety.

waking hours, his intellect is unclouded and unerring'[52] – he zig-zagged from initial support of the British declaration of war on Germany in 1939 to requiring individual demonstrations of *satyagraha* against it in 1940, to a sudden decision that the British must be driven forthwith from the subcontinent, come what may, in 1942. The Quit India movement was imposed by Gandhi on a reluctant Congress leadership, which was not convinced by it. It was his final throw, and this time he not only called for a tax-strike, but accepted in advance that violence might break out. Riots erupted across the country, police stations were attacked, rail-tracks torn out.

For a wave of younger fighters, it was an insurrection for independence. But Congress had never prepared for one, indeed envisaged any such thing, and the Raj was now on a war footing – the Indian Army would swell to two million troops after 1939. The rebellion, without training or leadership, was put down with fusillades on the ground, strafing from the air, sixty thousand arrests, four thousand casualties. After the event, Gandhi would describe it as a calamity. His third and last campaign against British rule had ended in a practical failure as complete as that of the first two. By 1945 he was politically speaking a back number. Of the anti-colonial leaders of the twentieth century, few ended their careers with much glory, many among the ruins of their hopes or reputation: Nasser and Nehru broken by posturing and rout on the battlefield, Sukarno dying a prisoner in his palace, Ben Bella in exile and oblivion, Makarios his country truncated and occupied for the duration. An assassin's bullet spared Gandhi a comparable fate, embalming him in the martyr's death that by then he wanted. 'Had

---

52 *CWMG*, Vol 75, p. 177: 17 December 1941 [Vol 81, p. 384]; Vol 72, p. 193: 22 June 1940 [Vol 78, p. 349].

that stupid and shortsighted fellow allowed Gandhi to live his natural life, and die a natural death like all mortals', wrote one compatriot, 'he would have, I am quite certain, grown weightless like, say, Vinoba Bhave', his futile epigone.[53] The verdict is overstated. But the kernel of truth in it is written in what would become of his ideals today: a face on a banknote.

Satyagraha had not been a success: each time Gandhi had tried it, the British had seen it off.[54] His great achievement lay elsewhere, in the creation of a nationalist party, whose road to power forked away in another direction. For in the end independence did not come from passive resistance, let alone sexual abstinence, individual or universal. It was the result of two other dynamics. The first was the broadening of the electoral machinery first introduced by the British in 1909, and expanded in 1919. Designed originally as a safety-valve to coopt a native elite, and disregarded by Congress as long as Gandhi set its course, it remained the stand-by of the Raj as nationalist pressures mounted. In 1929, a scheduled ten-year review of the system set in place after the First World War fell due, and undeflected by civil disobedience, issued after three Round Table Conferences in the Government of India Act of 1935, the longest bill ever passed by the British Parliament. At the outset, Halifax had made a public promise of eventual Dominion status, lifting India to the position of Australia or Canada as a self-governing state within the Empire, date unspecified.

---

53 Manmath Nath Gupta, *Gandhi and His Times*, Delhi 1982, p. 294. Gupta was an Indian revolutionary who spent twenty years in British jails. His book contains a biting critique of Gandhi's positions on the Boer War and First World War: pp. 58–71.

54 For this pattern, see D.A. Low, *Britain and Indian Nationalism: The Imprint of Ambiguity, 1929–1942*, Cambridge 1997, pp. 180–181.

The Act, envisaging a federal constitution for the subcontinent integrating its areas of direct and indirect rule through negotiation with its princely rulers, was the fruit of Baldwin's acute anxiety to avoid 'another Ireland'.[55] It did not mention the term, to which Conservative backbenchers led by Churchill took strenuous objection, but made all legislative bodies – provincial and central – elective, and extended the franchise from six to thirty-five million voters. Arriving on the heels of Gandhi's retreat from political life in 1934, it cleared the way for elections in 1937 that delivered Congress victories across the country. By 1938, eight out of eleven provinces were under Congress rule, and party membership had soared from 470,000 in 1935 to 4.5 million.[56] The wine of electoral success had done what the water of non-violence had failed to do: give Congress a political weight and strength that neither rulers nor rivals could henceforward ignore. It would be the last time the party threw itself into a popular campaign with such vigour. Thereafter, its power essentially rested, as D.A. Low, one of the finest historians of India, has remarked, on mass approbation, not mobilization. But that would be enough. 'The consensus pursued by the high command in the 1930's', Ian Copland has written, 'was at the expense of important sections of Indian political society which were deliberately left out in the cold – the poor peasantry, the tribals, the factory workers, and the people of the [princely] states. The Congress' attitude to these groups was suspicious, resentful and above all paternalistic. Like the British Raj, the Congress high command believed it knew what was good for

---

55 Kenneth Middlemas and John Barnes, *Baldwin: A Biography*, London 1969, pp.

56 For the figures, see B.R. Tomlinson, *The Indian National Congress and the Raj, 1929–1942. The Penultimate Phase*, London 1976, p. 86. A change emphasized in D.A. Low, *Eclipse of Empire*, Cambridge 1991, pp. 94–100.

the Indian people, and like the Raj it did not suffer gladly those who defied its leadership'.[57] Once in office, its provincial governments often proved as repressive of labour or the left as the colonial authorities. The social forces they represented formed a conservative coalition, which neither required nor welcomed an awakening of the poor. The Raj was not threatened by any popular upheaval from them.

After 1937, that the horizon of electoral advance could only be some form of independence, which was now bound to come sooner or later, was obvious to all. But that the British remained determined to defer that resolution as long as they could, and retained the power and the will to stretch it out for quite some time, was equally clear. The Viceroy of the period, Linlithgow, hoped it could be indefinitely. Nehru thought independence would probably come in the 1970s.[58]

What changed these expectations overnight was a hammer-blow from outside. Supplying the force from which Congress had always shrunk, the Japanese Army swept through South-East Asia, knocking over French, Dutch and British positions within a few weeks of the start of the Pacific War. In February 1942 Singapore surrendered. By the first week of March, Rangoon had fallen. In April, Colombo was bombed, and Japanese planes were attacking ports south of Orissa. The effect in London was electric. Even Churchill now realized that political concessions could be needed to shore up the Raj, and Cripps was dispatched to reach a deal with the major parties in India,

---

57 Ian Copland, 'Congress Paternalism: the "High Command" and the Struggle for Freedom in Princely India', in Jim Masselos (ed), *Struggling and Ruling: The Indian National Congress, 1885–1985*, New Delhi 1987, p. 135.

58 C.S. Venkatachar, *Witness to the Century*, Bangalore 1999, p. 62, a senior civil servant who worked closely with Patel.

where he promised Dominion status at the end of hostilities, in exchange for full support to the war effort. 'It would be hypocritical to deny that the expediency of the moment has given British policy the air of a death-bed repentance', confessed *The Economist*.[59] Congress, emboldened by the turn of events, demanded immediate formation of an Indian government instead, and when the deal fell through, was pushed by Gandhi, who believed Japan would win, into Quit India.

That could be crushed. Yet the offer of proximate Dominion status, once made, was difficult to revoke. It had been conditional, and the condition not met. But withdrawal of it became politically impossible, not least because of the formation of a Provisional Government of Free India by Bose, who had escaped arrest in Calcutta and via Russia and Germany had reached Singapore, where he took command of the 60,000 Indian prisoners of war there as a Japanese ally. Under Bose, the dedication and courage of Indian National Army – uniting Hindu, Muslim and Sikh combatants – in battle against the British in Manipur and Burma won such widespread admiration in India, not least from Gandhi himself, that prosecution of its officers had to be dropped after the war in the face of angry mass demonstrations. Superior American might could overpower Tokyo by 1945. But the blows the Japanese Army and its allies had dealt European colonialism in South-East and South Asia were irreparable. At war's end, the independence of the subcontinent was a foregone conclusion. What was not decided was the form it would take.

---

59 'Message to India', 14 March 1942.

2.
Partition

By 1945, the era of Gandhi was over, and that of Nehru had
begun. It is conventional to dwell on the contrasts between the
two, but the bearing of these on the outcome of the struggle
for independence has remained by and large in the shadows.
Nor are the contrasts themselves always well captured. Nehru
was, of course, a generation younger; of handsome appearance;
came from a much higher social class; had an elite education in
the West; lacked religious beliefs; enjoyed many a paramour. So
much is well known. Politically more relevant was the peculiar
nature of his relationship to Gandhi. Inducted into the national
movement by his wealthy father, a pillar of Congress since the
1890's, he fell under the spell of Gandhi in his late twenties, at a
time when he had few political ideas of his own. A decade later,
when he had acquired notions of independence and socialism
Gandhi did not share, and was nearly forty, he was still writing
to him: 'am I not your child in politics, though perhaps a truant
and errant child?'[1] The note of infantilism was not misplaced;

---

[1]   Judith Brown, *Nehru: A Political Life*, New Haven 2003, p. 87.

the truancy, in practice, little more coquetry. Like so many others, dismayed by Gandhi's scuttling of Non-Cooperation in 1922, in despair at his fast against Untouchable electorates in 1932, baffled by his reasons for suspending Civil Disobedience in 1934, he nevertheless each time abased himself before his patron's judgement.

Sacralization of the national movement? 'I used to be troubled sometimes by the growth of this religious element in our politics', but ' I knew well that it supplied a deep inner craving of human beings'. The fiasco of Non-Cooperation? 'After all, he was the author and originator of it, and who could be a better judge of what it was and what it was not. And without him where was our movement?' The fast to death at Poona? 'For two days I was in darkness with no light to show the way out, my heart sinking when I thought of some results of Gandhiji's action...And then a strange thing happened to me. I had quite an emotional crisis, and at the end of it I felt calmer and the future not so dark. Bapu had a curious knack of doing the right thing at the psychological moment, and it might be that his action – impossible as it was to justify from my point of view – would lead to great results'. The claim that God showed his displeasure with Civil Disobedience by visiting an earthquake on Bihar? He was 'dragged from the anchor of his spiritual faith' by Bapu's announcement, but deciding his action was right, 'somehow managed to compromise'. For 'what a wonderful man Gandhi is, after all'. All these avowals date from 1936, when Nehru was politically more radical – 'inclining to a communist philosophy' – than at any other time in his career. By 1939 he was simply exclaiming: 'India cannot do without him'.[2]

---

2 *An Autobiography*, London 1936, pp. 72, 374, 84–85, 370–371, 507–508, 591; Brown, *Nehru*, p. 133.

In this degree of psychological dependence, different strands were intertwined. Quasi-filial infatuation with Gandhi was not peculiar to Nehru, but the depth of parental affection – withheld, often with extraordinary harshness, from his own children – Gandhi felt for Nehru was unique. Mingled with these emotional bonds were calculations of mutual interest. So long as he operated in the ambit of Congress, Gandhi could count on Nehru never taking adult political issue with him, while as Gandhi's favourite, Nehru could count on prevailing over rivals to head Congress, and after independence, to rule the country. Still, was there not all the same an intellectual gulf between them? In one fundamental respect, there was indeed. Nehru never had any time for Gandhi's extraterrestrial dreams or earthly archaisms. He was a strictly intramundane believer in the benefits of industry and modernity. Yet this was not a dividing-line that mattered much, so long as state power was out of reach. Where the political outlook of the national movement under the Raj was concerned, there was far less distance between mentor and pupil than the contrast in their cultural backgrounds might have suggested.

Gandhi did not claim much book learning. In London, he had found his legal text-books full of interest – a manual on real-estate 'read like a novel' – but Bentham too difficult to understand. Tracts by Ruskin and Tolstoy were a revelation in South Africa. In prison in India he came to the conclusion that Gibbon or Motley were 'inferior versions of the *Mahabharata*', and he could have written *Capital* better than Marx.[3] What fixed his attention were the short list of works he had read by the time of *Hind Swaraj*, and a limited number of Hindu classics.

---

3   *An Autobiography*, Boston 1957, pp. 80, 46; *CWMG*, Vol 25, p. 128: 11 September 1924 [Vol 29, p. 134]; Louis Fischer, *The Life of Mahatma Gandhi*, New York 1950, p. 331.

By the time he left South Africa, his basic ideas about the world were essentially complete, undergoing little or no further development. Not in more books, but in himself lay truth. 'I have searched far and wide for another individual, placed in comparable circumstances, who has used the first person singular with such unabashed abandon as M.K. Gandhi', wrote an Indian critic, warning of the dangers of 'such cocksureness in an ill-stocked mind'.[4]

Nehru, on the other hand, had enjoyed a higher education Gandhi lacked, and an intellectual development not arrested by intense religious belief. But these advantages yielded less than might be thought. He seems to have learnt very little at Cambridge, scraping a mediocre degree in natural sciences that left no trace thereafter, did poorly in his bar exams, and was not much of a success when he returned to practice law in the footsteps of his father. The contrast with Bose, a brilliant student of philosophy at Cambridge, who was the first native to pass the exams into the elite ranks of the Indian Civil Service and decline entry to it on patriotic grounds, is striking. But an indifferent beginning is no obstacle to subsequent flowering, and in due course Nehru became a competent orator and prolific writer. What he never acquired, however, was a modicum of literary taste or mental discipline. His most ambitious work, *The Discovery of India*, which appeared in 1946, is a steam-bath of *Schwärmerei* with few equals in the period. It would be unfair to compare Nehru to Ambedkar, intellectually head and shoulders above most of the Congress leaders, in part due to far more serious training later on at the LSE and Columbia, to read whom is to enter a different world. But *The Discovery of India* – not to speak of its predecessor *The Unity*

---

4   T.K. Mahadevan, 'Foreword' to Gupta, *Gandhi and His Times*, p. v.

of India – illustrates not just Nehru's lack of formal scholarship and addiction to romantic myth, but something deeper, not so much an intellectual but a psychological limitation – a capacity for self-deception with far-reaching political consequences.

'India was in my blood and there was much in her that instinctively thrilled me', he told his readers, 'She is very lovable and none of her children can forget her wherever they go or whatever strange fate befalls them. For she is part of them in her greatness as well as her failings, and they are mirrored in those deep eyes of hers that have seen so much of life's passion and joy and folly and looked down into wisdom's well.'[5] Not all of *The Discovery of India* is of similar quality. But the Barbara Cartland streak was never far from the surface: 'Perhaps we may still sense the mystery of nature, listen to her song of life and beauty, and draw vitality from her. That song is not sung in the chosen spots only, and we can hear it, if we have ears for it, almost everywhere. But there are some places where it charms even those who are unprepared for it and comes like the deep notes of a distant and powerful organ. Among those favoured spots is Kashmir, where loveliness dwells and an enchantment steals over the senses.'[6] A mind capable of prose like this was unlikely to show much realism about the difficulties facing the national movement.

When Gandhi was blackmailing Ambedkar to submit to the demand that Untouchables be treated as loyal Hindus within the caste system, rather than pariahs excluded from it, Nehru had uttered not a word in solidarity or support for Ambedkar. Gandhi was fasting, and even though it was on a 'side-issue', as Nehru significantly dismissed it, that was

---

5   *The Discovery of India*, New York 1946, pp. 38, 576. Henceforward *DI*.
6   *DI*, p. 568.

enough. More was involved here, however, than simple unwillingness to differ with Gandhi on any issue in which he chose to take a political stand. Nehru, as he often confessed, was no believer: the doctrines of Hinduism meant little or nothing to him. But, in much the same artless way as Gandhi, he identified the religion with the nation, explaining that 'Hinduism became the symbol of nationalism. It was indeed a national religion, with all those deep instincts, racial and cultural, which form the basis everywhere of nationalism today'. By contrast Buddhism, though born in India, had lost out there because it was 'essentially international'.[7] Islam, not even born in India, was inevitably even less national.

It followed that the system Gandhi had always insisted was the foundation on which Hinduism rested, historically preserving it from disintegration, had to be presented in a roseate light. Caste had its tares, of course, as Gandhi too conceded. But in the larger view of things, Nehru explained, India had no reason to hang its head. 'Caste was a group system based on services and functions. It was meant to be to be an all-inclusive order without any common dogma and allowing the fullest latitude to each group'. Mercifully free from what had handicapped the Greeks, it was 'infinitely better than slavery even for those lowest in the scale. Within each caste there was equality and a measure of freedom; each caste was occupational and applied itself to its particular work. This led to a high degree of specialization and skill in handicrafts and craftsmanship', in a social order that was 'noncompetitive and nonacquisitive'. Indeed, far from embodying any principle of hierarchy, caste 'kept up the democratic habit in each group' (*sic*).[8] Later generations, hard

---

7   *DI*, p. 129.

8   *DI*, pp. 248–249, 211, 250, 253.

put to take in that Nehru could have composed such enormities, can point to other passages in which he added that 'in the context of society today' – as opposed to the (undated) past – caste had become a 'barrier to progress' that was no longer compatible with democracy, political or economic.[9] Untouchability, as Ambedkar would note bitterly, Nehru never so much as mentioned.

But it would be a mistake to think Nehru's embellishments of caste were tactical or cynical. They belonged to the same *Schwärmerei* as his discovery of the pluri-millennial 'impress of oneness' on the Indian character and the rest. History, Gandhi had written, was an interruption of nature. Its evidence was beside the point. What Gandhi had claimed for himself, Nehru generalized. 'What is truth? I do not know for certain', Nehru wrote in the same work, 'But truth is at least for an individual what he knows and feels to be true. According to that definition I do not know any person who holds to the truth as Gandhi does'. In the cause of the nation, 'Gandhi was always there as a symbol of uncompromising truth to pull us up and shame us into truth'.[10] With epistemological protocols like these, Nehru could perfectly well affirm the freedom and equality of caste on one page, and express a hope for its passing on the next.

If this was his view of the national religion and its core institutions, how did followers of the faith that was national neither in origin nor in extension figure in his outlook? Nehru's first real test as a political leader came with the elections of 1937. No longer an adjutant of Gandhi, who had withdrawn to the wings after 1934, he was President of Congress in the year of its triumph at the polls, and the formation of its first regional

---

9 *DI*, p. 254.

10 *DI*, p. 362

governments. Crowing over the results, Nehru announced there were now only two political forces that mattered in India: Congress and the British government. There is little doubt that, with fateful self-deception, he believed this. In fact, it was a confessional victory. By this time, the membership of Congress was 97 per cent Hindu. Across India it could not even find candidates to run in close to 90 per cent of Muslim constituencies. In Nehru's own province, Uttar Pradesh, then as now the most populous in India, Congress had swept the board of Hindu seats. But it had not won a single Muslim seat. Still, relations between the Muslim League and Congress had not been bad in the electoral campaign itself, and when the results were in, the League sought a coalition between the two parties that would give it some representation in the Ministry now to be formed in Lucknow. At Ņehru's behest – 'I am personally convinced that any kind of pact or coalition between us and the Muslim League will be highly injurious'[11] – it was curtly told to dissolve itself into Congress if it wished any such thing. Ambedkar would describe the mentality of high caste Hindus as monopolist. Whatever the validity of such a generalization, obviously questionable, there could be no doubt that the central ideological tenet of Congress was its claim to a monopoly of legitimacy in the struggle for independence.

Why then had ordinary Muslims failed to vote for it in sufficient numbers along with all other Indians? Nehru's answer was that they had been misled by a handful of Muslim feudatories, and would rally to Congress once they had understood the social interests they shared with their Hindu brethren. Under

---

11 Letter to Pant, 30 March 1937: see Bimal Prasad, 'Congress versus the Muslim League 1935–1937', in Richard Sisson and Stanley Wolpert (eds), *Congress and Indian Nationalism*, Berkeley-Los Angeles 1988, pp. 325–326, 329.

his leadership, a "Mass Contacts" campaign was launched to convince them of these. But unlike Bose, Nehru had little intuitive contact with the masses, and the effort soon fizzled. It was the last time he would ever engage in an attempt at mobilization from below. A year later, no longer president, he colluded with the ousting of Bose, in theory a fellow-fighter on the left of the party, but unlike him immune to the spell of Gandhi, and a rival capable of denying him the succession. Attacking Nehru for his desertion, Bose put it down, not to political ambition, but to weakness of character. He was still not an independent actor, remaining, in the matter-of-fact judgement of one historian, an 'utterly reliable' prop of the Old Guard within the party.[12]

After the outbreak of the Second World War, the Congress High Command instructed all its provincial governments to resign, in protest at the Viceroy's declaration of war on Germany without consultation with the people of India. The immediate result was to create a political vacuum, into which Jinnah, aware that London badly needed some show of loyalty in its major imperial possession, stepped with assurance. Declaring the end of Congress ministries a 'Day of Deliverance', he lost no time in expressing support for Britain in its hour of need, and winning in exchange its war-time favour. But he faced a difficult task. He was by now uncontested leader of the Muslim League. But the Muslim populations of the subcontinent were far from united. Rather they resembled a jigsaw-puzzle whose widely scattered pieces could never be got to fit together. Historically, the cultural and political heartland of the Muslim elite lay in UP, where the League was strongest, but only a third of the population answered the call of the muezzin. Far away to the west, Sindh, Baluchistan and the North-West Frontier

---

12 Brown, *Nehru*, p. 134.

were overwhelmingly Muslim. But conquered late by Britain, they were a rural backwater dominated by local notables who did not speak Urdu and felt no allegiance to the League, which had scarcely any organizational presence in them. In two of the richest provinces of India, widely separated from each other, Punjab and Bengal, Muslims formed a majority – narrow in the former, and more substantial in the latter. But in neither was the League a dominant force.

In Punjab, it was insignificant. There the Unionist Party that controlled the province was a coalition of big Muslim landlords and rich Hindu Jat farmers, both with strong ties to the Army, and loyal to the Raj.[13] In Bengal, on the other hand, where the League was led by aristocratic landowners owning huge estates in the east of the province, it was a mass peasant-based party, the KPP, that made the political running. Thus wherever observers looked, at provincial level the Muslim League was weak, either locked out of power by Congress in Hindu-majority areas, or bypassed by rival formations in Muslim-majority zones. What saved it was Jinnah's standing as the only Muslim politician capable of operating with sufficient skill and brio at an All-India level to make the Unionist, KPP and other leaderships willing to let him represent them in negotiations with the British at the centre, while they held onto their provincial fiefs. This fragmented and disarticulated landscape was one of the reasons for the hubris of Congress after the 1937 elections. To its High Command, the League looked like a spent force that might now be ignored, while the various local Muslim parties were coopted or picked off at leisure.

---

13 For a comprehensive historical analysis of this configuration, and its background, see Tan Tai Yong, *The Garrison State: The Military, Government and Society in Colonial Punjab, 1849–1947*, New Delhi 2005, pp. 240–280.

The War, however, would rapidly alter this configuration. The British, who in the aftermath of the Mutiny had regarded Muslims as the most dangerous of their subject populations in India, had by the turn of the century come to view them as the safest counterweight to the rise of Hindu nationalism, granting them separate electorates to ensure they would not automatically form a bloc with it in a common struggle against the Raj. But they did not want communal violence to upset their claim to have brought law and order to the subcontinent, or to antagonize unduly the more powerful Hindu community, with its own numerous friendly landlords and traders. So they were careful not to be too one-sided in their favours. But once the Congress governments had abdicated, and the League was offering public support to the war effort, Jinnah became the interlocutor of choice for the Viceroy. Though thoroughly secular in outlook and mode of life, for decades he had been rebuffed by a Congress whose sociological reality he could see all too clearly. In composition it was essentially a Hindu party, as Nehru senior – more lucid, or simply more candid, than his son – had noted, whose rule at the centre was unlikely to be more congenial to Muslims than it had proved in the provinces.

Hitherto, aware of the weakness of his base and unwilling to be pinned down by it, he had avoided formulating any too specific demands of the Raj. Now, emboldened by the turn of events, he unveiled a new programme. At Lahore in 1940, he announced that there were two nations, not one, in the subcontinent, and that independence would have to accommodate their coexistence in a form that gave autonomy and sovereignty to those areas where there was a Muslim majority, as constituent units within any future constitution. The wording of the resolution adopted at his behest by the League was deliberately ambiguous: it spoke of constituent 'states' in the plural, not the singular, and did not mention the word Pakistan – which Jinnah subsequently complained was being pinned on him by Congress. Behind the vagueness of the phrasing lay the insoluble dilemma he faced.[14] More or less homogeneously Muslim majority areas might be plausible candidates for their own independence. But did areas with less overwhelming majorities have the same potential? Above all, if majority areas seceded from a putative India, what would happen to the minorities – Jinnah's own political base – they left behind? Would these not need the shelter of an encompassing union of some kind, in which the Muslim majorities elsewhere could protect them from arbitrary exercises of Hindu will? Contemplating all these thorns, might not Jinnah himself be bluffing – floating unrealistic demands as bargaining counters, to get a realistic maximum? Many thought so at the time, and not a few since.

But whatever gloss might be put on the Lahore Resolution, it was now clear that independence was not in itself going to be any guarantee of that ageless unity of the nation on which the ideologues of Congress had so often dwelt. The threat to this posed by the stage at which rivalry between Hindu and Muslim political identities had reached was immediate and unmistakeable. What was Nehru's reaction? In a characteristic passage of his *Autobiography*, he had in 1935 dismissed any possibility of a Muslim nation in India: 'Politically, the idea is absurd, economically it is fantastic; it is hardly worth considering.'[15] In 1938, he informed an American audience 'there is no religious or

---

14   The commanding study of the problems Jinnah confronted, and the ways he tried to deal with them, remains Ayesha Jalal's *The Sole Spokesman: Jinnah, the Muslim League and the Demand for Pakistan*, Cambridge 1985, which rewrote the field.

15   *An Autobiography*, p. 469.

cultural conflict in India' – 'the tremendous and fundamental fact of India is her essential unity through the ages'.
Republishing his essay in 1941, after Lahore, he saw no reason
to revise his claim that 'the forces working for Indian unity are
formidable and overwhelming, and it is difficult to conceive
of any separatist tendency' – it was staring him in the face –
'which can break up this unity'.[16]

By 1945 Wavell – Commander-in Chief in India during
the War – was Viceroy and knew the imperial game was up,
remarking: 'Our present position in India is analogous to that
that of a military force compelled to retreat in the face of greatly
superior numbers'.[17] In June, Nehru and his colleagues were
released from prison, and in the winter provincial and central
elections were held, still on the suffrage of 1935. The result was,
or should have been, a cold douche for Congress. The Muslim
League had not dwindled or vanished. Jinnah had used the war
to build up its organization, increase its membership, create its
own daily, and gain a foothold in provincial governments from
which it had hitherto been excluded. Dismissed as a busted
flush in 1937, it won a landslide in 1945–46, taking every single
Muslim seat in the central elections and 89 per cent of them
in provincial elections. Its position in the Muslim community
now approached that of Congress in the Hindu.

From London, the Labour government despatched a
Cabinet Mission to negotiate a constitutional framework for

---

16 *The Unity of India*, pp. 14, 20, 21. In a foreword to the book, Krishna
Menon assumed responsibility for the selection of texts in it, suggest-
ing that difficulties of correspondence with Nehru, then in prison in
Dehra Dun, made it impossible for Nehru, to have any say in its con-
tents, entrusted by him to Menon. Nehru, however, made it quite clear he
was satisfied with the book when he saw it: *Selected Works of Jawaharlal
Nehru*, New Delhi 1978, Vol XI, p. 695.

17 *TOP*, Vol VIII, § 406, 7 February 1946, p. 796.

independence acceptable to all parties. The federal scheme it eventually proposed bore some resemblance to the arrangements vaguely evoked by Jinnah at Lahore. But though this time the positions of the League had stiffened considerably, both parties at first consented to the plan. Two weeks later, Nehru repudiated it, declaring Congress free to act as it pleased. It was his first purely individual decision as a political leader. Even his hard-line colleague Patel described it as 'emotional insanity', but once launched the torpedo could not be called back. In retaliation, Jinnah – who had always denounced any such thing as a reckless appeal to the mob – declared a Day of Direct Action to demonstrate that Muslim patience with a constitutional road was now over. A politician skilled in manoeuvre at elite level, he had no experience of mass action, or idea of how to direct or control it. Communal slaughter ensued in Calcutta. Initiated by Muslim thugs, it ended – inevitably, given the relative size of the two communities – with many more Muslims killed than Hindus.

At his wit's end, Wavell called an Interim Government into being, headed by Nehru as Prime Minister, Patel as Interior Minister, and – after an initial League boycott – Jinnah's deputy Liaquat Ali Khan as Finance Minister. Each party was determined to thwart the other. The League boycotted a Constituent Assembly composed of delegates nominated on the basis of the provincial election results, and therefore dominated by Congress, to which the government was in principle to be responsible; Congress blocked Liaquat's proposal for a wealth tax on the grounds that since most businessmen were Hindu, the measure would be an act of religious discrimination. Such was the situation when in February 1947, the Attlee government announced that India would have independence by June

1948, and dispatched Mountbatten to take over as Viceroy in charge of the handover.

With his arrival, imperial policy towards the religious divide in India came full circle. In the second half of the nineteenth century, Muslims were suspect to the Raj as first movers of the Mutiny, Hindus regarded as more dependable. In the first half of the twentieth, favours were reversed, as Hindu nationalism became the more assertive, and Muslim aspirations were patronized as a check to it. Now, on the last lap, London lurched violently back towards the political expression of the majority community as its privileged interlocutor. In 1947, the emotional intensity of the switch came from a sudden confluence of ideology, strategy and personality. The Labour regime in Britain viewed Congress as the Indian party closest to its own outlook; Fabian links with Nehru were long-standing. To sentimental affinity was joined national amour-propre. Britain had made of a dispersed subcontinent for the first time in its history a single political realm. For it to fissure at the moment of withdrawal would be to put a question-mark over what all right-thinking patriots, not least such products of an imperial education as Attlee, must regard with pride as the most remarkable creative achievement of their empire. If Britain had to leave India, India should be as Britain had forged it. Alongside such ideological investments in the unity of the subcontinent were considerations of a more material nature. Britain still had valuable possessions in Asia, not least in Malaya, the most profitable of its colonies and soon to be the theatre of a communist insurgency, which it was in no hurry to relinquish; while a short distance away from the North-West frontier lay the traditional bugbear of the Raj, now in the far more fearsome guise of the Soviet Union. Division of the subcontinent – the Chiefs of Staff were unanimous – could only play into the hands of the Russians. If the gates of South Asia were to be barred securely against Communism, the strategic interests not only of Britain, but also the West, required the bulwark of a united India.

All this indicated that the Muslim League, once a tactical expedient for the Raj, was now the principal obstacle to a satisfactory settlement of its affairs. Jinnah, personification of the difficulty it posed, could hardly expect the same treatment as the leaders of Congress, upholding the integrity of the heirloom to be bequeathed by Britain. But to this structural asymmetry was added the imbalance of an individual vainglory that fatally compounded it. We owe an indelible portrait of Mountbatten – that 'mendacious, intellectually limited hustler' – to Andrew Roberts.[18] Full of imaginary exploits from the back seat of his Cadillac in Colombo, as figurehead Commander of Allied Forces in South-East Asia, he arrived in Delhi overjoyed to be 'endowed with an almost heavenly power. I realised that I had been made the most powerful man on earth' (*sic*).[19] A grotesque of sartorial and ceremonial vanity – obsession with flags and froggings regularly displacing matters of state – Mountbatten had two over-riding concerns: to cut a figure fit for Hollywood as the last ruler of the Raj, and – above all – to ensure India would remain a Dominion within the Commonwealth. 'The value to the United Kingdom both in terms of world prestige and strategy would be enormous', he enthused.[20]

If the Raj had to be divided, it was the larger part – the larger, the better – that mattered for British purposes, so

18 'Lord Mountbatten and the Perils of Adrenalin', *Eminent Churchillians*, London, pp. 55–136.

19 Larry Collins and Dominique Lapierre, *Mountbatten and the Partition of India*, Vol I, New Delhi 1982, p. 25 – interview.

20 Alan Campbell-Johnson, *Mission with Mountbatten*, London 1953, p. 87.

conceived. To all the political reasons why Congress was now the preferred partner in planning the future of the subcontinent was further mixed a personal one. In Nehru, Mountbatten found delightful company, a social equal with a touch of the same temperament. Gandhi, who had always sought to remain on good terms with the British, had picked Nehru as his successor partly on the grounds that he was culturally equipped get on so well with them, as Patel or other candidates were not. Within weeks, not only was the Congressman fast friends with the Viceroy, but soon thereafter in bed with his wife, to the satisfaction of all concerned. The Indian state remains so prudish about the connubium that fifty years later it was still intervening to block the appearance of an American film touching on it, while its historians tiptoe round it. Affairs of the heart rarely affect affairs of state. But in this case the erotic ties of the triangle were, at the least, unlikely to tilt British policy towards the League. Diplomats are dismissed for less.

Even so, the language with which Mountbatten and Nehru, echoed by Attlee, regularly described Jinnah, at a time when Britain was ostensibly still seeking to bring the parties in India together, and Congress to lead a united country to independence, is arresting. For Mountbatten, Jinnah was a 'lunatic', a 'bastard', a 'clot', a 'psychopathic case'; for Nehru, a 'paranoid' heading a party of 'Hitlerian leadership and policies'; for Attlee, 'that twister'.[21] Communal riots were raging in Punjab as Mountbatten arrived. Within a month he had decided that since the deadlock between Congress and the League could not be overcome, partition was inevitable. The agenda now became: how was the realm to be divided? Essentially, this came down

---

21 Jalal, *The Sole Spokesman*, p. 259; Desai, *The Rediscovery of India*, London 2011, p. 283.

to five questions. What was to happen to the two key provinces of Bengal and Punjab where there was a Muslim majority, but not of an overwhelming magnitude? How were the zones of princely rule, where neither Congress nor the League had any computable presence, to be allocated? Would there be any popular consultation, either about the principle of partition, or where its lines should lie? Who would superintend the process of division? Over what time-period would it be implemented?

At this point, the reckonings of Congress and the League changed places. The credibility of Congress's claim to represent the whole nation, the centre-piece of its ideology since the twenties, had crashed with the demonstration of the League's command of the Muslim electorate. But what was the League to do with its new-found strength? Six years after Lahore Jinnah had still not found any way to square the circle of sovereignty for Muslim-majority provinces with safeguards for Muslim minorities in Hindu-majority provinces. All that had happened was that the slogan of Pakistan, which he had rejected in 1943, had proved so popular among Muslims that, without clarifying it, Jinnah had made it his own, now claiming that the plural 'states' of the Lahore Resolution had been a misprint for 'state'. He seems to have calculated that the British, confronted with the incompatibility of League and Congress aims, would ultimately – taking their time about it – impose a confederation to their liking on the two parties, in which the Muslim-majority zones of the subcontinent would be self-governing, with a central authority weak enough not to impinge on them, but strong enough to protect Muslim minorities in self-governing Hindu-majority zones. In the event, the Cabinet Mission had produced a plan close enough to this vision.

But for Nehru, such a scheme was worse than partition, since it would deprive his party of the powerful centralized state to which it had always aspired, and he believed essential to preserve Indian unity. Congress had aways insisted on its monopoly of national legitimacy. That claim could no longer be sustained. But if the worst came to the worst, it was better to enjoy an unimpeded monopoly of power in the larger part of India than to be shackled by having to share it in an undivided one. So while the League talked of partition, Jinnah contemplated confederation; while Congress spoke of union, Nehru prepared for scission.[22] The Cabinet Mission Plan was duly scuppered. Everything then turned on how the spoils were to be distributed. The British still ruled: Mountbatten would do the distribution. Nehru could be confident of his favour, but not in advance be sure of the extent of it. For Mountbatten, paramount in importance was the objective of keeping whatever states were to emerge from the Raj within the re-labelled British Commonwealth. That meant they must accept independence as Dominions. The League had no objections. But Congress had since 1928 rejected, on principle, any submission of India to fabrications from London, expressly including future as a Dominion. For Mountbatten, this raised the unacceptable prospect of the lesser community, which he regarded as the principal culprit of partition, becoming a member of the Commonwealth, while the larger community, not only relatively blameless but of much greater strategic and ideological importance, remained outside it. How was this conundrum to be solved?

---

22 The best analysis of this final *chassé-croisé* is to be found in Asim Roy, 'The High Politics of India's Partition: the Revisionist Perspective', *Modern Asian Studies*, 24, 2, 1990, pp. 403–48, who is equally critical of both parties; reprinted in Hasan (ed) *India's Partition*, at pp. 125–131.

The answer came from the Father Joseph of the moment, V.P. Menon, a Hindu functionary from Kerala in the upper ranks of the imperial bureaucracy, working on Mountbatten's personal staff and a close confederate of Patel, the organizational strongman of Congress. Why not offer Mountbatten Indian entry into the Commonwealth, in exchange for a partition so point-blank that it would leave Congress in control not only of the far larger territory and population to which it was entitled by religion, but in swift command of the capital and the lion's share of the military and bureaucratic machinery of the Raj? As a final sweetener, Menon suggested throwing the princely states – hitherto left inviolate by Congress, and nearly equal in size and population to any future Pakistan – into the pot, as compensation for what would be foregone to Jinnah?[23] Patel and Nehru took little persuasion. If these assets were handed over within two months, the deal would be done. Informed of this breakthrough, Mountbatten was overjoyed, later writing to Menon: 'It was indeed fortunate that you were the Reforms Commissioner on my staff, and thus we were brought together into close association with one another at a very early stage, for you were the first person I met who entirely agreed with the idea of Dominion status, and you thought of the solution which I had not thought of, of making it acceptable by a very early transfer of power. History must always rate that decision very high, and I owe it to your advice.'[24] History would be less admiring than he supposed.

There was one last-minute hiccup. Due to present London's finalized plan for independence and partition to leaders of all the interested parties at Simla, Mountbatten had a 'hunch' that

23 Copland, *The Princes of India in the Endgame of Empire*, Cambridge 1997, pp. 253–254.

24 Leonard Mosley, *The Last Days of the British Raj*, London 1961, p.127.

he must show it in confidence to Nehru before any of the others saw it. Nehru's reaction was furious: the Plan did not adequately acknowledge that the Indian Union would be the successor state to the Raj, with all that went with such a position, and Pakistan a secession from it. The two were not to be put on the same footing. The Viceroy thanked his lucky stars for his intuition. Without it, he said, he and his men would have 'looked complete fools with the Government at home, having led them up the garden to believe that Nehru would accept the Plan', and 'Dickie Mountbatten would have been finished and could have packed his bag'.[25] But the invaluable Menon was to hand, and the day was saved when he redrafted the Plan to Nehru's satisfaction. In the first week of June, Mountbatten announced that Britain would transfer power at what he himself would describe as 'the ludicrously early date' of August 14. The logic of such a rush was plain, and in speaking of it Mountbatten did not beat about the bush. 'What are we doing? Administratively it is the difference between putting up a permanent building, a nissen hut or a tent. As far as Pakistan is concerned we are putting up a tent. We can do no more'.[26]

The rules laid down for the territorial division of the Raj excluded any consultation with its population. Instead, the legislative assembly of each province would decide to which state it wished to belong, with three exceptions. In Punjab and Bengal, the assembly would be given the option of dividing the province; and in the North-West Frontier, uniquely, there would be a referendum. Religion automatically assigned all but these to India or Pakistan. In Punjab, the Muslim majority in the assembly voted for Pakistan, the Hindu and Sikh minorities

---

25 Campbell-Johnson, *Mission with Mountbatten*, p. 89.
26 *Mission with Mountbatten*, London 1952, p. 87.

for India. Bengal was another matter. With nearly four times
the population, it was not landlocked, had a stronger common
identity, a richer cultural-intellectual tradition and more
advanced politics under the Raj. There, unlike Punjab, division was not a foregone conclusion. In the Hindu community a
movement led by Bose's brother Sarat, and in the Muslim community by the the local head of the League, Suhrawardy, joined
forces to call for United Bengal as an independent state, adher-
ing neither to India nor to Pakistan. Mountbatten wanted only
two Dominions in the sub-continent, though if it was difficult
to avoid, did not rule out a third. Jinnah, to his credit, said he
would not oppose a unitary Bengal. Leading a violent attack on
the idea in Bengal was the ancestor of today's BJP, the rabidly
confessional Hindu Mahasabha. The first mass upsurge of
Indian nationalism had come over Curzon's division of Bengal
in 1905, Hindu activists leading the revolt against it. Now the
roles were reversed, Hindu chauvinists insisting that Bengal be
partitioned on religious lines.

What was Nehru's position? India should take as much territory as it could get: if religion was a lever to that end, so be
it. Mountbatten reported a formal exchange with Suhrawardy
to the Governor of Bengal with the revealing phrase: 'I warned
him that Nehru was not in favour of an independent Bengal
unless closely linked to Hindustan (*sic*), as he felt that a partition now would anyhow bring East Bengal into Hindustan in
a few years'.[27] East Bengal is today's Bangladesh. For Nehru,
Bengal could remain united only if it belonged to India. But as
matters stood, the Congress High Command took the view that
'the independence of Bengal really means in present circumstances the dominance of the Moslem League in Bengal', and

---

27   *TOP*, Vol X, London 1981, § 462, p. 850: 16 May 1947.

the party rallied behind the Mahasabha, with joint meetings whipping up Hindu demands for its partition, Gandhi in support.[28] When the question was put to the Bengal Assembly, the vote was 126 to 90 in favour of unity. But when representatives of West and East cast ballots separately, as they were required to do, the West voted for partition, the East against it, and divided along religious lines Bengal duly became. The prediction of its Governor had proved accurate: 'Bengal will be sacrificed on the altar on Nehru's all-India outlook'.[29]

What of the one province whose population would actually be allowed to express their views on partition? The North-West Frontier was an oddity in the political chequerboard. Since the thirties, the settled zone – mainly Pathan – had seen the rise of a strong Muslim anti-colonialist movement, the Red Shirts, dedicated to a non-violence akin to, but independent, of Gandhi's

---

28 For critical accounts of the the role of Congress, see Leonard Gordon, 'Divided Bengal: Problems of Nationalism and Identity in the 1947 Partition', in Hasan (ed), *India's Partition,* pp. 306–313; and Joya Chatterji, *Bengal Divided: Hindu Communalism and Partition, 1932–1947,* Cambridge 1994, pp. 128, 144, 148, 250–3. Bidyut Chakrabarty, *The Partition of Bengal and Assam, 1932–1947. Contour of Freedom,* London 2004, is more defensive, offering lame justification of the 'religious sensibilities' requiring Congress to join with the Mahasabha in carving up the province, where Hindus were 'left no option but to press for partition': pp. 21–25. But even this exercise in official apologetics contains much that is damaging to its High Command – Birla, in favour of dividing Bengal as early as 1942, for example convincing Gandhi to veto a Hindu-Muslim coalition in Calcutta on the grounds that it would harm Marwari business interests: pp. 133–134.

29 *TOP,* Vol X, § 554, p. 1025: 28 May 1947. See Mieville to Abell: 'In the course of talk I had with Nehru last night, I asked him how he viewed the discussions now going on about an independent Bengal. He reacted strongly and said there was no chance of the Hindus agreeing to put themselves under permanent Muslim domination, which was what the proposed agreement really amounted to. He did not, however, rule out the possibility of the whole of Bengal joining up with Hindustan': Vol X, § 552,. 1013: 28 May 1947.

Hindu version. Led by a local landlord, Badshah Khan, it was affiliated to Congress, though by no means always in line with it. The tribal areas of the province, tightly controlled by the British, were kept off-limits to nationalist organization of any kind. Backed by Badshah Khan and the Red-Shirts, Congress had won a majority in the provincial elections of 1946. But when Nehru paid a visit in the autumn of that year, after the mutual pogroms in Calcutta, he was given a hostile reception in Peshawar, and worse with an incursion into the tribal zone. Historically, the Muslim League had always been very weak in the province, but as communal tensions rose across Northern India, it started to gain strength not only in the settled but the tribal zones, mounting demonstrations and boycotts against the local Congress ministry, and a massive rally when Mountbatten descended on Peshawar.

The Red Shirts had campaigned on the platform of a united India, and won a majority for Congress in the provincial assembly. But the North-West Frontier was 95 per cent Muslim, and geographically separated from the rest of the Congress-held subcontinent. After his visit, Mountbatten judged it too risky to proceed as elsewhere, by a simple decision of the provincial assembly: some kind of verification of popular opinion as to its future would necessary. Congress, opposed to any kind of referendum on partition, accepted one in the NWFP only on condition that it exclude any option for independence – even then, Nehru still expressing a hope to Gandhi that 'we can get out of it'.[30] For Badshah Khan, however, Congress's acceptance of partition was a betrayal of innumerable promises to do no such thing, and the exclusion of any choice for an independence in a referendum, the one option that his movement could now

---

30 Pyarelal, *Mahatma Gandhi: The Last Phase*, Vol II, Ahmedabad, p 270.

realistically stand for, a double betrayal. The Red Shirts boy-cotted the referendum, nearly half the voters following them, the rest rallying behind the League to give an overwhelming majority for joining Pakistan.

Strategic considerations no doubt played a role in Congress calculations: a detached borderland did not fit the strong compact India had in mind for the moment, even if the NWFP, as the Red Shirts bitterly pointed out, was far closer to Delhi than East Bengal was to Karachi within the impending Pakistan. But the unceremonious abandonment by Congress of the only Muslim province where it had twice won an – albeit borrowed – electoral majority answered, obviously enough, to the religious nature of the partition that it denied and the League proclaimed. Nehru's own reception there was probably also decisive. In the judgment of the best – Indian – histo-rian of the Red Shirts, 'Nehru was both notoriously vain and in possession of a considerable temper, and he is unlikely ever to have forgiven the Pathans for the humiliation he suffered at the hands of the Tribes... He returned to Delhi having given up on the Frontier'. Badshah Khan, for whom the worst blow came where he had least expected it, is supposed to have told his fellow-pacifist Gandhi: 'You have thrown us to the wolves'.[31]

The rest of the Raj was divided without even this iota of popular consent. The provincial assemblies nominally entrusted with partition had not been elected on the issue. Many indeed, as in the North-West Frontier, had been elected in opposition to it. They themselves represented only a frac-tion – less than one out of seven – of the population. Partition was imposed from above, deliberately circumventing any

---

31 Mukulika Banerjee, *The Pathan Unarmed: Opposition and Memory in the North-West Frontier*, Oxford-Santa Fe-Karachi 2003, pp. 188, 189.

expression of a democratic will. 'Never before in South Asian history', has written one trenchant local observer, 'did so few divide so many, so needlessly'.[32] The validity of that adverb would need unpacking. But 'murderously' could have been written without fear of qualification. In Sumit Sarkar's no less bitter words: 'A "bloodless" winning of independence would be accompanied by an unimaginably bloody communal carnage.'[33] The number of those who died when the division was enforced has never been accurately calculated. But few estimates place it at less than a million. The number of those uprooted, fleeing to lands they never knew, was anywhere from twelve to eighteen million: the largest avalanche of refugees in history.

Though communal killings occurred across north India, the major flash-points were the two divided provinces, Punjab and Bengal. But there was a significant difference between them. Huge waves of refugees criss-crossed in Bengal. But, comparatively speaking, the expulsions occurred with relatively little violence. In Punjab, on the other hand, not only were the bonds of a common culture weaker, but the province had long been poisoned by its role as supplier of *soldateska* to the Empire. In a traditionally militarized ambience, teeming with veterans of imperial war and repression, religious hostilities exploded in reciprocal massacre.[34] Sikh vigilantes, from the community with most reason – no more than 13 per cent of the population – to fear from what was coming, pre- armed by their religion with *kirpans*, and backed by the rulers of Patiala

---

32 Aijaz Ahmad: ' "Tryst with Destiny:": Free and Divided', in *Lineages of the Present*, London-New York 2000, p. 5, radicalizing Mushirul Hasan (ed), *India's Partition: Process, Strategy and Mobilization*, New Delhi 1993, p. 41.

33 *Modern India, 1885–1947*, New Delhi 1983, p, 408.

34 See the conclusion to Yong, *The Garrison State*, pp. 308–309.

and Kapurthala, were already starting their deadly work before actual partition.[35] Four and a half million Hindus and Sikhs were driven out of their homes to East Punjab, five and a half million Muslims to West Punjab, in a communal inferno.

The trail to this conflagration was set in motion on July 7, when London dispatched the future British law lord Cyril Radcliffe to Delhi to determine the boundaries of the two states, India and Pakistan, to be given independence on August 15, five weeks away. He knew nothing of the subcontinent. But there already existed a detailed plan to divide it, drawn up in 1946 by none other than V.P. Menon and another Hindu bureaucrat, B.N. Rau, who would play a scarcely less fateful role in events under way. Radcliffe adhered closely to it. But not closely enough for Mountbatten. Officially supposed neither to exercise any influence on Radcliffe, nor to have any knowledge of his findings, he intervened – probably at the behest of Nehru – behind the scenes to alter the award. Like most senior judges of the day – in the age of Denning, Widgery or Hutton, has it changed that much? – Radcliffe could be bent, not to money, though he was well rewarded, but to power. Mountbatten had little difficulty getting him to change his boundaries to allot two pivotal Muslim-majority districts in Punjab to India rather than, as originally, to Pakistan: one controlling the only access road from Delhi to Kashmir, the other containing a large arsenal.

Radcliffe finalized his Award on August 12, exiting rapidly back to England before it was announced. He made sure to leave no incriminating evidence for posterity, destroying all his papers. Today, only Auden's feeble lines preserves his

---

35 For this, see Ishtiaq Ahmed, *The Punjab Bloodied, Partitioned and Cleansed*, Karachi 2012, pp. 539–540, to date the most comprehensive study of what befell the province, whose author is a Swedish citizen.

memory. Mountbatten, well aware of what was impending, timed announcement of the Radcliffe Award thirty-six hours after India and Pakistan had received their independence. It is still customary, at least in Britain, to praise the Labour government for its emancipation of the subcontinent after the war – the finest hour, in the view of a recent writer, in the career of Clement Attlee.[36] The reality is that the transfer of power put through Parliament in the first week of July 1947, amid an outpouring of self-congratulations on all sides, was literally breakneck: not for those who voted it, but those who suffered it. For partition to have any chance of being carried through peacefully or equitably, at least a year – the year London had originally set as the term of the Raj – of orderly adminstration and preparation was needed. Its conveyance within six weeks was a sentence of death and devastation to millions.

The British Empire bequeathed a series of partitions: Ireland, Palestine, India, Cyprus. But though colonial principles of divide and rule played a role in each, the cases were not the same. Ultimate architect of division in Ireland and Cyprus, ultimately indifferent to it in Palestine, when its time was up in the subcontinent British imperialism did not favour partition. But when London and Delhi decided they could not prevent it, they made of a setback to colonial amour-propre a human catastrophe. The avidity of Congress for the prize money of an instant division was the local motive of the disaster. But this was the party to it that could at least could be sure that it would thereby gain the instruments and accoutrements of sole power in a preponderant domain. Its aim was cold-blooded, in context rational. But Congress did not possess the means to

---

36 David Marquand, *Britain since 1918: The Strange Career of British Democracy*, London 2008, p. 129.

realize its goal. That Britain, still in command of the only army and bureaucracy across the Raj, retained. What prompted it to inflict partition on its subjects overnight? The bauble of a title to save its face: for Empire, now read Dominion. The spirit of the transaction was perfectly expressed in its finale. There would be no British responsibility for the consequences. Having lit the fuse, Mountbatten handed over the buildings to their new owners hours before they blew up, in what has a good claim to be the most contemptible single act in the annals of the Empire.

In the ensuing chaos, Congress made good a primary objective. To inheritance at midnight August 15 of successor status to the Raj, with its seat at the UN, and control of the capital and three-quarters of the territory and population of British India, would be added a still greater share of its arsenal. Fourteen out of twenty armoured regiments, forty out of forty-eight artillery regiments, and twenty-one out of twenty-nine infantry regiments fell into its grasp, plus the larger part of the air-force and navy. Of the 160,000 tons of ordinance legally allotted to Pakistan, no more than 23,000 ever reached it.[37] There remained the question of how the territorial assets left outstanding by the grant of simultaneous independence were to be distributed – the two-fifths of the subcontinent ruled by princes over whom Britain had juridically been only suzerain. In theory they were free to choose their future. In practice, if they declined voluntarily to join one or other of the two new states, none had the means to resist annexation. The overwhelming majority – some 550 out of 560 – were Hindu potentates ruling Hindu populations, and were swiftly rounded up for India by Mountbatten, with assurances from Patel and Menon that their

---

37 Stephen Cohen, *The Pakistan Army*, Berkeley 1984, p. 7; Ian Talbot, *Pakistan: A Modern History*, New York 1988, p. 99.

opulence would not be touched by the new authorities. In the two cases where the ruler was Muslim and the overwhelming majority of the population Hindu, Congress settled the matter by force. In Junagadh, a peninsula lying across the water from Sind, whose prince opted for accession for Pakistan on August 15, it sent in troops without further ado to secure the state for India. The vastly larger state of Hyderabad, where the notoriously benighted Nizam wished to maintain his independence, was seized with an invasion a year later. Post-partition, both actions enjoyed the support of the majority of the local population, and could be defended on grounds of self-determination, as conforming to its wishes.

In Kashmir, the boot was on the other foot. There a Hindu ruler – rivalling the Nizam in obscurantist tyranny – lorded it over a population that was overwhelmingly Muslim. The largest princely state in the subcontinent, it had been sold by the East India Company to a Dogra adventurer in the 1840's, whose descendants presided over a sectarian regime whose senior officers and bureaucrats were exclusively Hindu, and down to 1920 there was a death penalty for Muslim peasants, most living in abject misery, should they kill a cow. In that decade, the first political organization in the state – unsurprisingly a 'Muslim Conference' – came into existence, headed by a local teacher, Shaikh Abdullah. Within a few years, it had changed its name to a 'National Conference', and by 1944 had adopted a social programme to the left of either Congress or the Muslim League, drafted by Communists within the party, envisaging an independent Kashmir as an Asian Switzerland. Its position, however, was weakened by collaboration with the Maharajah's regime in the name of support for the British war effort, and then by an unsuccessful attempt to redeem itself by campaigning for his ouster, which landed Abdullah in jail in 1946. In the southern part of the state, Jammu, where the Muslim majority was not so large, and a substantial Dogra population provided the backbone of Hindu rule, inter-communal tensions had for some time given a split-away force, reviving the banner of a Muslim Conference, the upper hand over the National Conference.

At partition the Maharajah, seeking to preserve his autocracy, declared neither for India nor Pakistan. His realm was 77 per cent Muslim, but Kashmir itself was 92 per cent Muslim, and shared a border with Pakistan but none with India. If religion and geography were to determine its allocation, there could be no ambiguity where it would belong. It had never, however, occupied a significant position in Jinnah's political outlook. The 'six provinces' that by the end of the war he was demanding for Pakistan included Assam, with a large Hindu majority, but not Kashmir. The extraordinary inattention and ineptitude of his handling of it, once Partition came, was the fruit of long-standing limitations. Jinnah was more quintessentially a lawyer than any Congress leader; more committed to constitutional methods of advance; and during the war tactically much closer to the British, for whom meddling with local rulers that had shown their loyalty to the Raj was out of bounds. Congress itself had long made scant attempt to build grassroots organizations in the princely states, the Muslim League none. In 1947 a blinkered legalism seems to have prompted Jinnah to the naïve calculation that the right of the Nizam to hold onto land-locked Hyderabad, in the middle of the Deccan, would be compromised by any challenge to the right of the Maharajah to dispose of Kashmir, as if there were any realistic chance of the former not being absorbed by India, whatever the juridical niceties. Cultural formation also played its part. Historically a product of Bombay, whose main following was in the central plains of UP, Jinnah's familiarity with the northwest of the subcontinent was distant and weak. Islam was no reliable bridge. Abdullah, a pious Muslim who prided himself on Quranic lore, regarded Jinnah as little better than an atheist, while a Muslim League mission to Kashmir reported that the locals were so heterodox as to be little better than pagans.[38] As Pakistan loomed, Jinnah's mind was elsewhere.

The opposite was true of Nehru. Though himself born and raised in UP, his ancestors had come from the Hindu elite of Kashmir, offering sentimental investment in a region with which he otherwise he had little contact. First arriving there for a bear hunt in his late twenties, he did not set eyes on the region again till 1940. But when he did so, he commemorated the experience in a dithyramb of sexualized gush to embarrass the lowest tourist brochure. 'I wandered about like one possessed and drunk with beauty, and the intoxication of it filled my mind', he reported. 'Like some supremely beautiful woman, whose beauty is almost impersonal and above human desire, such is Kashmir in all its feminine beauty of river and valley and lake and graceful trees…sometimes the sheer loveliness of it was overpowering and I felt almost faint. As I gazed at it, it seemed to me dream-like and unreal, like the hopes and desires that fill us and so seldom find fulfilment. It was like the face of a beloved that one sees in a dream and fades away on awakening'. Happily, no such thing. His strophes concluded: 'Kashmir calls back, its pull is stronger than ever, it whispers its fairy magic

---

38 Alastair Lamb, *Incomplete Partition: The Genesis of the Kashmir Dispute, 1947–1948*, Hertingfordbury 1997, p. 98; Ian Copland, 'The Abdullah Factor: Kashmiri Muslims and the Crisis of 1947', in D.A. Low (ed), *The Political Inheritance of Pakistan*, New York 1991, p. 223.

to the ears, and its memory disturbs the mind. How can they who have fallen under its spell release themselves from this enchantment?'[39]

How indeed. Alongside such fantasies were more material considerations. For Congress, as for British military planners after the war, Kashmir was a strategic redoubt commanding the approaches to Central Asia. Still more crucial, however, was its importance as an ideological prize. If it went to India, it would demonstrate that Congress had built, as it had always said it would, a secular state in which a Muslim province could take its place among Hindu provinces, unlike the confessional state of Pakistan that had so gratuitously destroyed the natural unity of the subcontinent. Nehru, for whom its future was a matter of 'intimate personal significance', made no secret of the intensity of his feelings to Mountbatten, breaking down in front of Patel and weeping that Kashmir meant more to him than anything else, adding to Edwina that 'Kashmir affects me in a peculiar way – like music sometimes or the company of a beloved person'.[40] Later he would simply cry out 'I want Kashmir'. In June he was already supplying Mountbatten with a memorandum explaining that its accession to India would be the 'normal and obvious course' after Partition, and that it would be 'absurd to think that Pakistan would create trouble if this happens'.[41]

In Kashmir itself, trouble came of its own accord. It did not take long before the communal violence which erupted over the partition of Punjab spread to Jammu. There Dogra ethnic cleansing started to drive out Muslims. Then a full-scale Muslim

---

39 *The Unity of India*, pp. 223, 240.
40 *TOP*, Vol XII, London 1983, § 302, p. 450: 1 August 1947; Philip Ziegler, *Mountbatten: The Official Biography*, London, 1985, p. 445.
41 *TOP*, Vol XI, London 1982, § 229, p. 448. The document was submitted on 17 June 1947.

rising against Hindu rule exploded in the western borderland
of Poonch. In the Valley, where Indian arms had been quietly
stock-piled, a battalion materialized from Patiala. Finally,
inflamed by reports of massacres of fellow-Muslims in Punjab
and UP, and backed clandestinely – if haphazardly and incom-
petently, without heavy weapons or regular command – from
Pakistan, Pathan tribesmen poured down from the North-West
Frontier towards Srinagar, killing and plundering in their path,
the Maharajah fleeing to Jammu.[42] Once Pathan fighters were at
the gates of Srinagar, however, there was no time to lose if the
province was to be secured for India, and Delhi went into high
gear. There Mountbatten was now Governor-General of independent India, whose army – like that of Pakistan – remained
under the command of British generals. Acutely aware of the
importance of Kashmir for Nehru, Mountbatten had as early
as July 17, 1947, nine days after Radcliffe arrived to draw the
borders of Partition, been minuted by Menon that for India
to have access to it required passage through the district of
Gurdaspur in Punjab, the only overland route from Delhi
to Srinagar, and though it had a Muslim majority, Radcliffe
duly awarded it to India. There was never any doubt where
Mountbatten's sympathies lay.[43]

---

42 For a first-hand account of Pakistani involvement by one of the officers in
    charge of it, see (former major-general) Akbar Khan, *Raiders in Kashmir*,
    Karachi 1970, *passim,* and the documentation in Victoria Schofield,
    Kashmir in the Crossfire, London 1996, pp. 141–144; for slaughter and
    eviction of Muslims from Jammu, see (former editor of *The Statesman* in
    Calcutta) Ian Stephens, *Pakistan*, London 1963, p. 200, and (former UN
    Commissioner) Joseph Korbel, *Danger in Kashmir*, Princeton 1954, p. 92.

43 Contrasting it pointedly with Hyderabad, which was surrounded by
    Indian territory, Menon explained that Kashmir 'does not lie in the
    bosom of Pakistan, and and it can claim an exit to India, especially if a
    portion of the Gurdaspur district goes to East Punjab': *TOP*, Vol XII, §
    151, pp. 213–214 – 17 July 1947. Two weeks later, Mountbatten repeated

But legal cover was still required for military intervention by India, and on October 26 this was duly provided by
Menon, with a forged declaration of accession to India by the
Maharajah, supposedly brought back by him from Srinagar,
when in fact he was still in Delhi – a document recently 'discovered', on which the Indian state bases its entire claim to
Kashmir on it, but was unable to produce for half a century. In
reality the Maharajah, now a panic-striken fugitive in Jammu
and in no position to decline protection from Delhi, was perfectly willing to sign on the dotted line, but the Congress high
command, fearing Srinagar was about to fall, could not wait for
this formality.[44] Patel air-lifted troops into the city, and under
its British commanders, Mountbatten supervising operations,
the Indian Army swiftly took possession of most of Kashmir.[45]

---

to the Nawab of Bhopal and the Maharajah of Mysore that 'Kashmir was
so placed geographically that it could join either Dominion, provided
part of the Gurdaspur District was put into East Punjab by the Boundary
Commission': *TOP*, Vol XII, § 335, p. 509 – 4 August 1947.

44 Alastair Lamb's meticulous analysis of these events has not been shaken:
Incomplete Partition, pp. 114–178.

45 Stephens, invited to dinner with Mountbatten and his wife on the
evening of 26 October, noted afterwards: 'I was startled by their one-
sided verdicts on affairs. They seemed to have become wholly pro-Hindu.
The atmosphere at Government House that night was almost one of war.
Pakistan, the Muslim League and Mr Jinnah were the enemy. This tribal
movement into Kashmir was criminal folly. And it must have been well
organized. Mr Jinnah, Lord Mountbatten assured me, was waiting at
Abbottabad, ready to drive in triumph to Srinagar if it succeeded. It was
a thoroughly evil affair. By contrast, India's policy towards Kashmir, and
the princely states generally, had been impeccable. After the meal Lord
Mountbatten took me aside. As editor of an important paper I should
know the facts fully. Because of the Pathan attack, the Maharajah's formal
accession to India was at that moment being finalised. Subject to a plebiscite, this great State, its inhabitants mainly Muslim, would now be legally
lost to Jinnah. The Pakistanis had been crazy to accept the accession of
Junagadh. Indian troops were to be flown into Kashmir at once; arrangements had been made. This was the only way to save Srinagar from sack by

When Jinnah belatedly attempted a counter-intervention by the Pakistani Army, Auchinleck – Commander in Chief in Delhi – flew in to instruct his opposite number in Karachi, Messervy, that all British officers would have to resign, decapitating its command structure, if it made any move into Kashmir, which had legally acceded to India. Jinnah desisted. The Valley was handed to India on a British plate.

Still, it remained all too obvious that a province with an overwhelming Muslim majority had been acquired by force and – as would in due course become clear – fraud. Even the Labour government in London, preeminently well-disposed to Congress, expressed unease at the upshot, Attlee finding it a 'dirty business'. There was trouble too at the UN. The back-dated instrument of accession justifying Indian seizure of Kashmir, that could not be found after the event, was an embarrassment that apologists have since only worsened with bed-time stories that present Menon, on the correct date, waving the document in triumph to Manekshaw – the general who quarter of a century later, wanted India to finish off Pakistan altogether – with a triumphant cry of 'Sam, we have got it ', as if the fate of

---

ruffianly tribesmen'. Stephens, after remarking that Mountbatten 'manifestly banked on hustling *The Statesman* into complete support', writes: 'I was flabbergasted', for 'the whole concept of dividing the subcontinent into Hindu-majority and Muslim-majority areas, the basis of the June 3 plan, seemed outraged. At a Hindu Maharajah's choice, but with a British Governor-General's backing, three million Muslims, in a region always considered vital to Pakistan if she were created, were legally to be made Indian citizens. I said little, except for expressing doubts whether a plebiscite would prove readily feasible'. When Stephens published an editorial expressing his misgivings about the operation on October 28, he was summoned within a few hours by a furious Mountbatten and 'during the ensuing interview *The Statesman* was in effect threatened with death, on the Indian Cabinet's behalf, unless it adopted a more pro-Indian line': *The Horned Moon*, London 1953, pp. 109–110, 114.

five million people were a lottery ticket.[46] But the *ex post facto* assent of the Maharajah – himself summarily put out of the way once the province was safely in Delhi's hands – was no better defense, since India had famously brushed aside princely decision in favour of popular preference to take over Junagadh and Hyderabad. There remained, however, a third claim: that in Kashmir the popular will itself, embodied in Abdullah's National Conference, wanted integration with India. There is little reason to doubt that Nehru, believing Abdullah a political fellow-spirit, persuaded himself of this. Abdullah had indeed followed the Maharajah in approving accession to India, and the latter once coralled, was installed by Delhi as Prime Minister of Kashmir

But the option – temporary, as it turned out – of a leader and the mood of the people were not the same thing. Abdullah was a popular politician, then and later, in the Valley of Kashmir, but never an uncontested one. His National Conference faced fierce competition from the Muslim Conference that had split from it, and neither party had any mass organization comparable to Badshah Khan's Red Shirts, which had dominated the North-West Frontier since the early thirties. Yet when the chips were down in a plebiscite there, religious identity had trumped political allegiance, and the region voted for Pakistan. Abdullah's hand was weaker than Badshah's. That Delhi itself rapidly realized this is plain from what followed. Believing it

---

46 Prem Shankar Jha, *The Origins of a Dispute: Kashmir, 1947*, New New Delhi 2003, p 71. Even such a staunch apologist for New Delhi as Srinath Raghavan, a former Indian Army officer, author of a book that is a prolonged hymn to the strategic sagacity of Nehru, has felt obliged to discount this tale, in the course of complaining that the question of the authenticity of the instrument of accession has 'resulted in a literature out of all proportion to the importance of the matter', and burying it in a footnote: *War and Peace in Modern India*, London 2010, p 108. For Manekshaw in 1971, see Indira Gandhi's account to Tariq Ali, *The Duel: Pakistan on the Flight Path of American Power*, New York 2008, p. 200.

could count on a favourable vote, India officially promised a referendum to show that Kashmiris had rallied to it by their own free will, not simply at a ruler's whim. Their intelligence reports soon disabused the Congress leaders of this notion. By the summer of 1949, one of these reported from a tour of Indian-held territory that it was 'mid-summer madness to believe we can win a plebisicite'. Within another year Patel was writing to Nehru: 'It appears that both the National Conference and Sheikh Sahib [Abdullah] are losing their hold on the people of the Valley and are becoming somewhat unpopular... In such circumstances I agree with you that a plebiscite is unreal'.[47] Three years later, Abdullah's use had come to an end, and he was thrown into jail for conspiring against the state. No referendum would ever take place.

The concluding act of Partition was a military conquest of familiar stamp: territorial expansion by force of arms, in the name of national integration. Nothing in the outlook of the Congress high command, or traditional pattern-books of nationalism, was inconsistent with it. But what, it may be asked, of Gandhi? Did principles of non-violence and harmony between faiths distance him from the lunge for Kashmir? Far from it. 'What is the reason for our fighting in Kashmir? I consider I barbarous for the tribal raiders to have attacked Kashmir; we had to send an army to fight them', he told a prayer meeting. 'The simple fact is that Pakistan has invaded Kashmir. Units of the Indian Army have gone to Kashmir but not to invade Kashmir'. What if war broke out between the two new states? 'Do I imagine that several crores of Muslims in India will be loyal to India and fight against Pakistan? It is easy to pose such questions but difficult to answer them... If they later betray you, you

---

47 Durga Das (ed), *Patel's Correspondence*, Ahmedabad 1971, Vol I, pp. 286, 317.

can shoot them. You may shoot one or two or a certain number (*sic*). Everyone will not be disloyal'. What of the province itself? 'To whom does Kashmir belong? Right now I shall say it belongs to the Maharajah because the Maharajah still exists. In the eyes of the Government the Maharajah is still the legitimate ruler. Of course if the Maharajah is a wicked man, if he does nothing for the people, I think it is for the Government to displace him. But so far no such eventuality has arisen'. Abdullah? 'I have not the slightest doubt that if we show the least bit of slackness over Kashmir, Hyderabad and Junagadh are going to meet the same fate. Sheikh Abdullah is a brave man. But one wonders whether he may not betray in the end'. Prophetic words. Those who would in due course jail the traitor? 'The government is composed of patriots and no one will do anything that is in conflict with the interests of the country'.[48]

In the ranks of such patriots, none showed less trace of slackness than Sardar Patel, Minister of Interior. In a 'marvellous and deeply touching speech before officers and men of the Royal Indian Air Force on 1 October 1948', as a centenary volume of his writings describes it, Patel reported: 'While people talk of our failing to follow Gandhiji's teachings, I wish to give you one example which I remember from his conversation. When Srinagar was touch and go, when we wanted to put our Army in Srinagar and when the Air Force was asked to carry the Army and its requirements quickly, they did it with wonderful speed; and if we had been late by twenty-four hours, the whole game would have been lost. *That is the work which you have done, which is written in letters of gold in the history of Freedom.* We are proud of you. But what Gandhiji said to me

48 *CWMG*, Vol 90, p. 267: 20 December 1947; p. 298: 5 December 1947; p. 346: 2 January 1948; p. 460: 20 January 1948; p. 514: 28 January 1948; p. 529: 29 January 1948. [Vol 98, pp. 85, 113, 160, 275, 322, 336.]

was: "I feel so proud when I hear the noise of those aeroplanes. At one time I was feeling very miserable and oppressed when I heard this. But when this Kashmir operation began, I began to feel proud of them and every aeroplane that goes with materials and arms and ammunition and requirements of the Army, I feel proud'". (italics in original)[49]

Patel himself, who held that 'what nature and God had intended to be one on no account can be split in two for all times', had wider aims in view, as these were recalled by the admiring British Air Marshall who served under him: 'if all the decisions rested on me, I think I would be in favour of extending this little affair in Kashmir to a full-scale war with Pakistan… Let us get it over with once and for all and settle down as a united continent'.[50] Congress had accepted Partition as the price of a strong centralized state in which it could be sure of a monopoly of power, but in the mind of its top leaders it was a temporary concession. The party's resolution of June 5 1947 that formally agreed to partition made its position very clear. 'Geography and mountains and the sea fashioned India as she is, and no human agency can change that shape or come in the way of her final destiny' – least of all 'the false doctrine of two nations'.[51] Mountbatten had engineered point-bank Partition with the same end in mind, saying explicitly that this would 'give Pakistan a greater chance to fail on its demerits', and so was in the best interests of India, because a 'truncated Pakistan, if conceded now, was bound to come back later'.[52] In September,

---

49 *Sardar Patel: In Tune with The Millions*, Vol II, Ahmedabad 1975, p. 318.

50 Sucheta Mahajan, *Independence and Partition: The Erosion of Colonial Power in India*, New Delhi 2000, p. 342; B. Krishna, *Sardar Vallabhbhai Patel: India's Iron Man*, New Delhi 1996, p. 397.

51 Victoria Schofield, *Kashmir in the Crossfire*, London 1996, p. 131.

52 *TOP* X, § 147, p. 251ff: 15 April 1947, 10 May 1947.

Auchinleck reported to London: 'The present Indian Cabinet are implacably determined to do all in their power to prevent the establishment of the Dominion of Pakistan on a firm basis'.[53] Nehru, who had for decades denied there was any possibility of an independent Muslim state in the subcontinent, repeatedly expressed his confidence that Pakistan was such a rickety structure – by October it was in his eyes 'already a tottering state' – that it had no chance of surviving.[54] The delusions of the Congress nationalism reshaped by Gandhi to Hindu specifications died hard.

Only outside Congress was there lucidity. Predictably, of those who would go on to construct the Indian state, Ambedkar alone was early on clear-sighted enough to see that self-determination could not be denied Muslims if they wanted it, and to propose a rational solution for it. In 1944, at a time when the very idea of it was taboo in Congress, and still little more than a vague slogan in the Muslim League itself, he published the only serious work on the issue which would determine the outcome of the struggle for independence. *Pakistan or Partition of India*, whose references range from Renan to Acton to Carson, from Canada to Ireland to Switzerland, stands as a devastating indictment of the intellectual poverty of Congress and its leaders.[55] Critical of Muslim introversion, alert to Savarkar's *Hindutva*, contemptuous of the myths of pan-religious amity, Ambedkar

---

53 John Connell, *Auchinleck*, London 1959, pp. 920–921.

54 *Selected Works of Jawaharlal Nehru* (ed S. Gopal), Second Series, Vol 4, pp. 270–271. In words so exactly repeating Mountbatten's formulation as to make clear the understanding they shared: 'We expected that partition would be temporary, that Pakistan was bound to come back to us': Leonard Mosley, *The Last Days of the British Raj*, London 1961, p. 248.

55 A shorter first version of this work had appeared as *Thoughts on Pakistan* in late 1940, in response to the resolution adopted by the Muslim League at Lahore.

did not advocate separation of the two communities, but he proposed referenda to determine popular wishes and in the event that Muslims insisted on it, sketched the boundaries he thought might ensue. After Partition, he would call for a division of Kashmir to allow its Muslim-majority zone, including the Valley, to join Pakistan.

The condition of Ambedkar's sanity was that he had broken with Hinduism. The condition of Nehru's obduracy was that he had not. When in the summer of 1945 an emissary of the Communist Party, the one other force in the subcontinent that understood something of the principles of self-determination, appealed to him to accept the prospect of Pakistan, he was told that was impossible because of the strength of Hindu opinion in Congress.[56] Three years later, Nehru would show what that attachment meant. When the Indian Army took over Hyderabad, massive Hindu pogroms against the Muslim population broke out, aided and abetted by its soldiers. On learning something of them, the figurehead Muslim Congressman in Delhi, Maulana Azad, then Minister of Education, prevailed on Nehru to let a team investigate. It reported that at a conservative estimate between twenty-seven to forty thousand Muslims had been slaughtered in the space of a few weeks after the Indian take-over.[57] This was the largest single massacre in the

56 Benjamin Zachariah, *Nehru*, London 2004, p. 123; brief but on the whole acute, this début by a young scholar is now perhaps the best critical study of its subject. Between the first and second edition of Ambedkar's work, the CPI came out with a clear position on the legitimacy – as distinct from desirability – of a demand for Pakistan, and more generally of rights to self-determination in the subcontinent, with the publication of Gangadhar Adhikari's *Pakistan and National Unity* in 1942, for which see *Remembering Dr Gangadhar Adhikari: Selections from his Writings*, Part II, New Delhi 2000, pp. 12–50.

57 See Omar Khalidi (ed), *Hyderabad: After The Fall*, Wichita 1988, pp. 95–99; and A.G. Noorani, 'Of a Massacre Untold', *Frontline*, 3 March

history of the Indian Union, dwarfing the killings by the Pathan raiders en route to Srinagar which India has ever since used as the *casus belli* for its annexation of Kashmir.

What action did Nehru, who on proclaming victory in Hyderabad had announced that 'not a single communal incident' had marred the Indian triumph, take? He suppressed the report, and at Patel's urging cancelled the appointment of one of its authors as ambassador in the Middle East. No word about the pogroms, in which his own troops had taken eager part, could be allowed to leak out. Twenty years later, when news of the report finally surfaced, his daughter banned any publication of the document as injurious to 'national interests', faithful to her father's definition of them. Had he not said 'the Congress is the country and the country is the Congress'? Such was the way the borders of contemporary India were finally completed.

The struggle for independence from the Raj, like every major anti-colonial movement, drew on profoundly impressive human energies – great courage, devoted organization, selfless sacrifice, political and moral imagination. Viewed historically, there was never any doubt that it would bring imperial rule by Britain to an end. That, after all, was the common fate of all European colonies after the Second World War. India was not ahead of other British possessions in the advance towards it. Ceylon had universal suffrage already in 1931, Burma its own Prime Minister by 1937. In the Dutch and French empires, Indonesia and Vietnam declared independence two years before India did so, in the teeth of military assault from Gurkha and Punjabi troops despatched there in imperial solidarity by

---

2001. Both authors append sections from the original Sundarlal Report. Noorani writes of the pogroms: 'This is a truth which hardly any Indian scholar has deigned to admit to his day' – dared would perhaps be the more appropriate verb.

Mountbatten. As a theatre of conflict the subcontinent was on a different geographic and demographic scale. But these epic dimensions also explain why the transfer of power, when it came, was so unlike the ordeal in Indonesia or Vietnam. In the Dutch East Indies, the ratio of colonials to natives was 1:200; in Vietnam 1: 475. In the Raj it was 1: 3,650.[58] The British had no hope of holding on after 1945, as the French and Dutch fought to do.

But if the independence of the subcontinent was inevitable, was its division too? Over half a century later, the struggle against the Raj has generated a vast literature, within India and beyond it. But it is striking how rarely this issue is ever centrally or candidly confronted by it. The major question posed by the modern history of the region has yet to receive analytic treatment commensurate with it. Too much remains politically at stake in any of the possible answers. The standard nationalist version in India is that British policies of divide-and-rule were responsible for splitting the national movement and precipitating partition. Historically, British power had in truth always rested on divisions in the subcontinent. But confessional antagonisms between Hindu and Muslim communities were not, in the nineteenth century, a primary instrument of control, if only because they risked aggregating dangerously wide blocs of religious identity, at the expense of more favourably fragmented political, ethnic and linguistic units. The Raj preferred safer subdivisions. When modern nationalism started into being among Hindus, the British accommodated the initial Muslim reaction to it with alacrity, granting separate electorates. But after that, no Viceroy stoked religious tensions deliberately. For the British, the ideal arrangement was rather to be found in

---

58 Robin Jeffrey, 'Introduction: The Setting for Independence', in Jeffrey (ed), *Asia – The Winning of Independence*, London 1981, p. 5.

Punjab, the apple of the imperial eye: inter-confessional unity around a strong regional identity, loyal to the Raj, against which neither Congress nor Muslim League made any headway in the inter-war years,[59] During the Second World War, when Congress came out against participation in the conflict, the League was favoured. But once the war was over, Britain sought to preserve the unity of the subcontinent as its historic creation, and when it could not, tilted towards Congress far more violently than it ever had to the League. Popular conceptions in India blaming the creation of Pakistan on a British plot are legends.

If the Raj can be eliminated as an efficient cause of Partition, we are returned to the famous remark of a veteran of Non-Cooperation at the Round Table Conference of 1931: 'We divide and you rule'. The ultimate drivers of the split were indigenous, not imperial. How were they distributed? The official view in Delhi, shared across the political spectrum, has always been that it was Jinnah's personal ambition that fired Muslim separatism, destroying the unity of the national liberation struggle and wrecking what would otherwise have been its natural culmination in a single ecumenical state coinciding with the borders of the Raj and bearing the proud name of India. Like most politicians, Jinnah was certainly ambitious. But he was also an early architect of Hindu-Muslim unity; had little mass following down to the end of the thirties; and even when he acquired one, probably aimed at a confederation rather than complete separation. The division in the struggle for independence, when it came, was confessional, but it was not Jinnah who injected religion into the vocabulary and imagery of the national movement, it was Gandhi. That he did not do so in any sectarian spirit, calling on Muslims to defend the Caliph in the

---

59   See Ian Talbot, *Punjab and the Raj*, New Delhi 1988, pp. 80–141.

same breath as Hindus to restore the golden age of Rama, was of little consequence once he jettisoned mobilization against the British without regard for his allies in the common struggle. Non-Cooperation died as a campaign to evict the Raj. It lived on as an all but permanent description of political relations between the two communities it had once brought together. What remained was Gandhi's transformation of Congress from an elite into a mass organization by saturating its appeal with a Hindu imaginary. Here, unambiguously, was the origin of the political process that would eventually lead to Partition.

By the mid-thirties, Congress as a party was close to monolithically Hindu – just 3 per cent of its membership was Muslim. Privately, its more clear-sighted leaders knew this. Publicly, the party claimed to represent the entire nation, regardless of religious affiliation. The reality was that by the end of the thirties, it commanded the loyalty of an overwhelming majority of the Hindu electorate, but had minimal Muslim support. Since Hindus comprised two-thirds of the population, it was already clear that free elections on either an unaltered or universal franchise would deliver Congress absolute control of any future all-India legislature. Common sense indicated that from a position of such strength, it would be necessary to make every feasible concession to ensure that the quarter of the population that was Muslim would not feel itself a permanently impotent – and potentially vulnerable – minority. Ignoring every dictate of prudence and realism, Congress did the opposite. At each critical juncture, it refused any arrangement that might dilute the power to which it could look forward. In 1928, after having initially persuaded Congress to accept Muslim allocation of a third of the seats in a national legislature, Motilal Nehru's Report reduced it to a quarter, and Jinnah was shouted down for attempting to revert to the original agreement. In 1937, coalition government in UP was rejected, the Muslim League told to dissolve itself into Congress. In 1942, the Cripps Mission was rebuffed for allowing constituent units freedom to choose whether or not to join a future Indian union. In 1947, Nehru killed off the Cabinet Plan as a confederation for giving too much leeway to areas where the Muslim League was likely to dominate. The display of blindness was unvarying.

Generating it was a fatal mixture of social misperception, electoral architecture and historical mythology. Nehru believed, down to the end of the Second World War, that the Muslim League was a reactionary clique of big landlords with no significant popular base, that could be discounted as a political force in face of the huge electoral support enjoyed by Congress. There was truth in the comparison, but also illusion. Even at its height of triumph in 1937, Congress did not command any considerable Muslim electorate, while the League would soon remedy its weakness. But the hubris of success was such that Nehru could declare 'When I speak, I do not speak as an individual but I speak with the authority of the hundreds of millions of India', and claim 'there is hardly any national body in the world to match the Congress'.[60] Intoxication of this sort was fortified by what remains to this day the most damaging legacy of colonial rule: not the stoking of communal furies, but the introduction of first-past-the-post voting systems, converting plurality into monopoly representation at constituency level.[61]

---

60 *Selected Works*, Vol 8, p. 309; Vol 10, pp. 309.

61 This ingredient in the situation is regularly ignored in the literature. Meghnad Desai, rightly critical of the vices of 'majoritarian nationalism', notes the influence on Congress of British traditions of government, to which 'consociational' arrangements that might have averted Partition were alien. But he does not touch on the electoral system imported from Westminster as such: *Rediscovery of India* pp. 199, 264–265.

It was partly because even the British realized the dangers of this in India that they granted separate electorates as a limited safeguard for Muslim minorities. But the effect of the system would still be to inflate Congress victory at the polls far beyond its actual support, magnifying an already overweening sense of its dominance still further.

Finally, and most fundamentally, the ideology and self-conception of Congress rested on a set of historical myths that disabled it from taking any sober stock of the political problems confronting the struggle for emancipation from the Raj. Central to these was the claim that India had existed as a nation time out of mind, with a continuous identity and overarching harmony prior to the arrival of the British. Congress, in this outlook, was simply the contemporary vehicle of that national unity, in which differences of religious faith had never prevented ordinary people living peacefully side by side, under the aegis of enlightened rulers. Imperialism had sought to set community against community, and a handful of self-seeking Mulim politicians had colluded with it, but independence would show the world an India stretching from the North-West to the North-East Frontier Agencies, at one with itself, a democracy governed by a party in the tolerant traditions of the greatest emperors of its past, the modern expression of an ancient civilization six thousand years old.

Cleansed from this edifying vision were the obvious facts that variegated Hindu populations, which had never formed a subcontinental state of these dimensions, had for centuries been subject to Islamic conquerors, formed in a faith at virtually every point – not least in its attitude to idols – antithetical to their own. The practical necessities of rule might temper arrangements with the infidel – much subsequent idealization surrounding figures like Akbar, as ruthless as the rest of his line in dealing with Rajput or other native foes – but there was never any doubt which religion had the force of the sword behind it, nor that, as in every pre-modern society with more than one confession, sectarian clashes at ground level would punctuate the record.[62] Under the British the tables were turned, and it was plain which community now had the upper hand. For Congress to believe that such deep legacies of conquest and conflict, of sweeping inequalities of power and reversals of them, could be erased with a mythology of Mother India of whom it was the natural offspring, could only be self-deception on a heroic scale. The consequence was a fatal partisan arrogance. What need could there be to arrive at a *modus vivendi* with the Muslim League, when the party of Gandhi and Nehru already embraced every part of the nation? Broadly speaking, a level-headed Indian historian has written, 'it was the persistent Congress claim to speak for the whole country as the only alternative to British rule that precipitated the crisis and made Partition inevitable.'[63] On this evidence, had it acted more modestly and wisely, the subcontinent could have avoided the calamity of its division.

Yet, of course, it can be argued that no political force could have averted that division, so deep were the long-standing differences, and latent antagonisms, between the two major

---

62 See the verdict of Sanjay Subrahmanyam, and his documentation of it: 'Let us make no mistake, the mediaeval and early modern record of violence in India too is not a prepossessing one, making nonsense of claims of generalized non-violence or tolerance. In this India is no different from her neighbours at a very broad qualitative level'. 'Before the Leviathan: Sectarian Violence in Pre-Colonial India', in Kaushik Basu and Sanjay Subrahmanyam, *Unravelling the Nation: Sectarian Conflict and India's Secular Identity*, New Delhi 1996, p. 78.

63 Misra, *The Unification and Division of India*, p. 316.

religious communities of South Asia. This was the position of the original advocates of Pakistan, and has remained the stance of its spokesmen and rulers ever since, in a no less mythological and anachronistic vision of 'two nations' projected back to Mughal days or the mists of time.[64] For obvious reasons, it has never been acceptable to official Indian nationalism, where Muslims were canonically regarded as Hindus converted – under pressure – to Islam, whom culturally and ethnically little or nothing otherwise separates from their fellow-countrymen. Empirically, however, the case is not to be dismissed. For the subcontinent was not just the theatre of two major, incompatible religious systems, but of an imbrication of these with unequal political power, and to boot a recent dramatic reversal of the hierarchy of dominance between them. Could a secular nationalism ever have successfully unified two such communities of believers?

That was the original goal of Congress, when it was still an elite concern. But if Gandhi put paid to it, the question remains whether even without him, the logic of mass organization in populations as steeped in the supernatural as those of South Asia, would not have transformed Congress into the Hindu party it became. For everywhere in the region, political awakening was intertwined with religious revival.[65] Well before Gandhi, the first stirrings of nationalism in Bengal were soaked with modernized Hindu appeals: its canonical work of

---

64 The extreme version propounds the fantasy of a separate 'Indus' civilization on the territory of today's Pakistan, from Mohenjo-Daro to the present: Aitzaz Ahsan, *The Indus Saga and the Making of Pakistan*, Karachi 1996, *passim*.

65 'The Indian identity was preceded by, or overlapped with the new Hindu identity; and almost overwhelmingly it was 'Hinduism' in the sense of a 'great tradition': G. Balachandran, 'Religion and Nationalism in Modern India', in *Unravelling the Nation*, p. 88.

fiction, Bankim Chatterji's *Anandamath*, whose poem invoking the goddess Durga would supply Congress with its anthem *Vande Mataram*, was already extolling wholesale destruction of Muslims as alien underlings of the British,[66] while the first political leader with an ardent national following, Tilak, was rousing his compatriots in Maharashtra with a new cult of the elephant-headed god Ganesh. In the background, already by the late nineteenth century communal riots were spreading. Nirad Chaudhuri's autobiography offers a vivid description of confessional antagonisms in turn of the century Bengal.[67] Prodromes like these might suggest that the chances of non-sectarian politics would have been cut off in due course anyway. Supporting evidence could be adduced from Ceylon, where the struggle for independence was led by a conservative elite that never wavered from a secular nationalism, offering an example of everything Congress had ceased to be, yet which within a

---

66 'For a long time we've been wanting to smash the nest of these weaver-birds, to raze the city of these Muslim foreigners, and throw it into the river – to burn the enclosure of these swine and purify Mother Earth again! Brothers, that day has come!' – 'Next the *santans* began to send a secret agent into every village. As soon as the agent entered a village and saw a Hindu he would say, "Friend, do you want to worship Vishnu?" He would collect twenty to twenty-five volunteers, and they would enter a Muslim village and set it on fire': *Anandamath, or, The Sacred Brotherhood*, Oxford-New York 2005, pp. 169,189. For a judicious analysis of this rabid text, see Tanika Sarkar, *Hindu Wife, Hindu Nation: Community, Religion and Cultural Nationalism*, New Delhi 2001, pp. 176–183. That Congress could have taken the book's war-cry for the party's own anthem speaks volumes for the Hindu insensibility of its leadership.

67 *The Autobiography of an Unknown Indian*, Berkeley-Los Angeles 1968, contains an unflinchingly self-critical analysis of the Hindu attitudes he grew up with: 'Heaven preserve me from the dishonesty, so general among Indians, of attributing this conflict to British rule, however much the foreign rulers might have profited by it'. Bankim Chatterji, he recalled, was 'positively and fiercely anti-Muslim. We were eager readers of these romances and we readily absorbed their spirit': pp. 225–232.

decade after independence had fallen into the hands of a vicious Sinhala-Buddhist chauvinism – the country itself renamed in its honour 'Holy' Lanka – plunging the island into decades of deadly communal warfare. On this reading, Gandhi's dictum 'If religion dies, then India dies' could be reversed.[68] The unitary India of his dreams died because the particularist religion of his forebears lived. Congress could then only superficially be held responsible for Partition, its successive blunders and hauteurs becoming effects, not causes, of a rift that was bound to split the Raj once the British left.

Such a conclusion, however, is not more palatable to polite opinion in India than the alternative. Confronted with the outcome of the struggle for independence, Indian intellectuals are caught in a fork. If Partition could have been avoided, the party that led the national movement to such a disastrous upshot stands condemned. If Partition was inevitable, the culture whose dynamics made confessional conflict politically insuperable becomes a *damnosa hereditas*, occasion for collective shame. The party still rules, and the state continues to call itself secular. The fork affords comfort to neither. It is no surprise the question it poses should be so widely repressed in India.

Historically, the larger issue could be held undecidable. What is not beyond accounting, however, is something else. Whether or not the Partition was bound to come, the plain truth is that the high command of Congress took scarcely any intelligent steps to avert it, and many crass ones likely to hasten it; and when it came, acted in a way that ensured it would take the cruellest form, with the worst human consequences. For even were a scission of the subcontinent foreordained by its deep culture, its manner was not. At the hour of division, the

---

68 *Harijan,* 18 May 1947, p 153. Omitted from *CWMG.*

political cupidity of Congress, in collusion with the dregs of the viceregal line, not only inflicted enormous popular suffering, which certainly could have been avoided, but compounded it with a territorial greed that has poisoned India's relations with its neighbour down to the nuclear stand-off today.

Though by then, as he remarked sadly, he had lost any real power, in his last months Gandhi tried to stem the tide of communal violence. Yet he cannot be acquitted of any connexion with it. He had consistently envisaged what might occur, and in advance accepted it. As early as *Hind Swaraj*, he had said that if his countrymen started to fight after the British withdrew, 'there can be no advantage in suppressing an eruption: it must have its vent. If therefore, before we can remain at peace, we must fight among ourselves, it is better that we do so'. In 1928 he wrote: 'I am more than ever convinced that the communal problem should be solved outside of legislation, and if in order to reach that state, there has to be civil war, so be it'.[69] In 1930: 'I would far rather be witness to Hindus and Mussulmans doing one another to death than that I should daily witness our gilded slavery'.[70] In April 1947, he told Mountbatten that 'the only alternatives were a continuation of British rule to keep law and order or an Indian bloodbath. The bloodbath must be faced and accepted'. To an Indian journalist, he said he 'would rather have blood-bath in a united India after the British quit than accept partition on a communal basis'.[71] In the dénouement, the violence that *satyagraha* spared the British was decanted among compatriots, as Gandhi had said was preferable.

---

69 *Hind Swaraj*, p. 85. *CWMG*, Vol 36, p. 282: 29 April 1928 [Vol 41, p. 474].
70 *CWMG*, Vol 42, p 388: 11 Jan 1930 [Vol 48, p. 219].
71 Campbell-Johnson, *Mission with Mountbatten*, p. 52; Durga Das, *India from Curzon to Nehru and After*, London 1969, p. 239.

To his honour, when the pogroms erupted in 1947, he did what he could to prevent them, to good effect in Calcutta. But still trapped in the Hindu nationalism out of which he came, he cheered on the seizure of Kashmir, if more as a befuddled spectator than an effective agent in the final debacle. Few historical figures have been purer embodiments of Weber's ethics of conviction. Since those convictions were beyond earthly reason, he cannot be criticized for them. Nehru, not a spectator but an architect of the outcome, possesses no such exemption. Eager at all costs to enter his inheritance, confident that subtractions from it would only be temporary, his record falls under another jurisdiction: the ethics of responsibility.

3.

Republic

To hallow the solemn occasion, Nehru and his colleagues sat cross-legged around a sacred fire in Delhi while Hindu priests – arrived post-haste from Tanjore for the ritual – chanted hymns and sprinkled holy water over them, while women imprinted their foreheads with vermilion.[1] Three hours later, on a date and at time stipulated by Hindu astrologers, the stroke of midnight on 14 August 1947, Nehru – in defiance of any earthly notion of time, announcing that the rest of the world was asleep: London and New York were wide awake – assured his broadcast listeners that their 'tryst with destiny' was consummated, and had given birth to the Indian Republic.

After the ceremonies, came practical arrangements. Within a fortnight, a Constituent Assembly had appointed a committee to draft a Constitution, chaired by the Untouchable leader Ambedkar. After it had laboured for over two years, a charter of 395 articles was adopted, the longest of its kind in the world,

---

[1] See Tai Yong Tan and Gyanesh Kudaisya, *The Aftermath of Partition in South Asia*, London-New York, 2000, pp. 53–54.

which came into force on January 26 1950. The document drew on British, American and White Dominion precedents for an original synthesis, combining a strong central executive with a symbolic presidency, a bicameral legislature with reserved seats for minorities, a Supreme Court with robust provincial governments, in a semi-federal structure denominated a Union. Widely admired at the time and since, and not only at home, the Constitution has become a touchstone of what for many are the signature values of India: a multitudinous democracy, a kaleideoscopic unity, an ecumenical secularity.

There is always some gap between the ideals of a nation and the practices that seek or claim to embody them. The width of that, of course, varies. In the case of India, the central claim is sound. Since independence, the country has famously been a democracy. Its governments are freely elected by its citizens at regular intervals, in polls that are not twisted by fraud. Although often thought to be, this is not as such a unique achievement in what was once called the Third World. Ceylon and Malaysia, Jamaica and Mauritius, can match regular elections as independent states. What sets Indian democracy apart from these is its demographic and social setting. In sheer scale, it is unlike any other democracy in the world. From the beginning, its electorate was over twice the size of the next largest, in the United States. Today, at some 700 million, it is over five times larger. At the far top of the range in numbers, India is close to the bottom in literacy and poverty. At independence, only 12 per cent of the population could read or write. Comparable figures for Jamaica were 72 per cent, Ceylon 63 per cent, Malaya 40 per cent. As for poverty, per capita income in India today is still only about a sixth of that of Malaysia, a third of that of Jamaica, and not much more than half that of Ceylon.

It is these magnitudes that make Indian democracy so remarkable a phenomenon, and the pride of its citizens in it legitimate.

To be impressive, however, is not to be miraculous, as Indians and others still regularly describe the political system that crystallized after independence. There was never anything supernatural about it: terrestrial explanations suffice. The stability of Indian democracy came in the first instance from the conditions of the country's independence. There was no overthrow of the Raj, but a transfer of power by it to Congress as its successor. The colonial bureaucracy and army was left intact, minus the colonizers. In the mid–30's Nehru, denouncing the Indian civil service as 'neither Indian nor civil nor a service',[2] declared it 'essential that the ICS and similar services disappear completely'. By 1947 pledges like these had faded away as completely as his promises that India would never 'under any circumstances' become a Dominion. The steel frame of the ICS remained in place, untouched. In the last years of the Raj, its upper ranks had been Indianized, and there was no other corps of native administrators available. But if this was true of the bureaucracy, it was not of the army. Indigenous officers and soldiers had fought bravely, arms in hand, against the Raj in the ranks of the Indian National Army. What was to be done with them, once the British left? Their record a potential reproach to Congress, they were refused any integration in the armed forces of the former colonial power, veterans of domestic repression and overseas aggression fresh from imperial service in Saigon and Surabaya, that now became the military apparatus of the new order. Nor was there any purge of the police that had beaten, jailed and shot so many in the struggle for

---

2   *Toward Freedom: the Autobiography of Jawaharlal Nehru*, London 1934, p. 445. Reprinting the book after 1945, Nehru suppressed this phrase.

independence: they too were kept intact. For the Congress High Command, the priority was stability. These were the sinews of a strong state.

The legacy of the Raj was not confined to them. Alongside its machinery of administration and coercion, Congress inherited its traditions of representation. The Constituent Assembly that gave India its Constitution was a British-created body dating from 1946, for which only one out of seven of the subjects of the Raj had been allowed to vote. Once independence was granted, Congress could have called for new elections, with universal adult suffrage. No doubt fearing the outcome might be less convenient than the conclave to hand, in which since Partition it controlled 95 per cent of the seats, it took care not to do so. No election on an expanded franchise was held till 1951–1952.[3] The body that created Indian democracy was thus itself not an expression of it, but of the colonial restrictions that preceded it.[4] The constitution to which it gave birth,

---

3   Pointing out the practical difficulties caused by the size and illiteracy of the adult population, Ramachandra Guha makes clear that the officials in charge took the view that an election based on universal suffrage was impossible before 1951–1952, when 106 million voters cast a ballot, or some 45.7 per cent of the electorate: *India After Gandhi*, pp. 133–135. Whether this was the only reason why an election was so delayed is another question. What is not in doubt is that the Congress High Command decided to write a Constitution before consulting a democratic expression of the popular will, as it had Partition.

4   'A strikingly narrow body in terms of its social composition', Sunil Khilnani has written, 'the Assembly was dominated by the upper caste and Brahmanic elites within Congress', and produced a constitution that 'came to be perceived not as something that was constitutive of public life, but rather as akin to club house rules: a set of complicated procedures for regulating etiquette in a very narrow sphere of life, and which could be dispensed with', since 'the acquisition of mass democratic rights (the franchise) was not the product of popular action, and it therefore could not embody in any secure way the learning and memory that results from such action'. See 'The Indian Constitution and Democracy', in Zoya

moreover, owed the majority of its provisions to Westminster: some 250 out of its 395 articles were taken word for word from the Government of India Act passed by the Baldwin cabinet in 1935. But the most important segment of the umbilical cord attaching the Congress regime of the post-independence years to the arrangements of the Raj was the least conspicuous. A mere six articles out of nearly four hundred dealt with elections, but these laid down that victors would be those first past the post in any constituency.

Though the Raj had imported this British system into the subcontinent, confronted with intractable local problems it had on occasion contemplated alternatives, the existence of which could not altogether be excluded from the deliberations of the Constituent Assembly. Over the protests of the handful of Muslim members left in it, any idea of proportional representation was given short shrift, and an undiluted Westminster model adopted for the Lok Sabha.[5] The Anglophone provincialism of the Congress elite played its part in this. When the functionary responsible for detailed drafting of the Constitution, the legal bureaucrat Benegal Rau, a recent locum for Delhi in Kashmir, was dispatched on a fact-finding tour abroad, he visited just four countries: Britain, Ireland, Canada and the United States, all reassuringly first-past-the post save Ireland. There, however, De Valera told him that 'he would do away with proportional

---

Hasan, E. Sridharan and R. Sudarshan, *India's Living Constitution: Ideas, Practices, Controversies*, London 2002, pp. 71, 74, 77 – a judgement in many ways acute, if too categorical, for as the case of Japan shows, even a democracy conferred from above can take institutional hold in due course.

5   For a clear-eyed account of the imposition of FPP after independence, see E. Sridharan, 'The Origins of the Electoral System: Rules, Representation and Power-Sharing in India's Democracy', in *India's Living Constitution*, pp. 344–369.

representation in any shape or form. He preferred the British system as it made for strong government.[6] Efforts by Fianna Fail to strengthen its grip on the island that would mercifully be frustrated, but whose logic was readily understood by Congress. The last thing it wished was to weaken its monopoly of power in India. First-past-the-post had delivered what it wanted in the past. Why forego it in the future?

The consequences were central to the nature of the Indian democracy that emerged once elections were held. For twenty years, across five polls between 1951 and 1971, Congress never once won a majority of votes. In this period, at the peak of its popularity as an organization, its average share of the electorate was 45 per cent. This yielded it crushing majorities in the Lok Sabha, amounting just under 70 per cent of the seats in Parliament. In effect, the distortions of the electoral system meant that at national level it faced no political opposition. At state or district level, this did not hold. But there, the centre had powers that could deal swiftly with any local trouble. These too were heirlooms of the Raj, eagerly appropriated by Congress. Preventive detention dated back to a Bengal State Prisoners Regulation of 1818, and been a standard weapon of colonial rule. At Rau's instigation, approved by Nehru and Patel, the Constitution retained it, eliminating due process.[7] Intervention by the Viceroy to over-ride or overturn elected

<hr>

6   'Report by the Constitutional Adviser on his Visit to U.S.A., Canada, Ireland and England', in *The Framing of India's Constitution: Select Documents*, Vol III, Bombay 1967, p. 223.

7   For Rau's role, see Granville Austin, *The Indian Constitution: Cornerstone of a Nation*, Oxford 1966, pp. 102–104 ff. Invoking the lore of the Code of Manu and the *Arthasastra* of Kautilya, Rau once informed an audience that even 'if the parliamentary system in all its modern details' was not yet present in ancient India, 'we may perhaps say that the essential conception was familiar': *India's Constitution in the Making*, Bombay-Calcutta-Madras-New Delhi 1960, pp. 317–319.

governments in the provinces was authorized by the hated
section 93 of the Government of India Act of 1935. At the last
minute, the same powers now reappeared in Article 356 of the
Constitution, transferred to the President of the Republic, in
practice a place-holder for the Prime Minister. Nehru and Patel
had wasted no time in showing the uses of the first, sweeping
Communist leaders and militants into jail across the country
within a few months of independence. Resort to the second
came within months of the adoption of the Constitution, when
Nehru demanded and obtained the head of the Chief Minister
in Punjab, a Congressman he regarded as insubordinate, over
the opposition of the newly installed President himself. In
Kerala, where the Communist governments were intermittently
elected, President's rule was imposed five times, from 1959
onwards. By 1987 there had been no less than seventy-five of
these take-overs by the centre, affecting virtually every state in
India. The representative institutions of Indian democracy were
thus from the start anchored in a system of electoral distortion,
and armour-plated with an ample repertoire of legal repression.

Still, limits to liberty such as these have never been peculiar
to India. In one degree or another another, they are familar elsewhere. All liberal democracies are significantly less liberal, and
considerably less democratic, than they fancy themselves to be.
That does not cancel them as a category. There is no reason to
judge India by a higher standard than is complacently accepted
in older and richer versions. The explanation of democratic
stability in so infinitely much poorer and more populous a
society is only to a secondary extent to be found in institutional
restrictions common enough in the species. It lies in a far larger
enabling condition. To see what this might be, a truly distin-
guishing feature of Indian democracy – one that sets it apart

from any other society in the world – needs be considered. In India alone, the poor form not just the overwhelming majority of the electorate, but vote in larger numbers than the better off. Everywhere else, the ratio of electoral participation is, without exception, the reverse – nowhere more so, of course, than in the ·Land of the Free. Even in Brazil, the other large tropical democracy, where voting – unlike India – is technically compulsory, the index of ballots cast falls as income and literacy decline.

Why then has the sheer pressure of the famished masses who apparently hold an electoral whip-hand not exploded in demands for social reparation incompatible with the capitalist framework of this – as of every other – liberal democracy? Certainly not because Congress ever made much effort to meet even quite modest requirements of social equality or justice. The record of Nehru's regime, whose priorities were industrial development and military spending, was barren of any such impulse. No land reform worthy of mention was attempted.[8] No income tax was introduced till 1961. Primary education was grossly neglected.[9] As a party, Congress was controlled by a coalition of rich farmers, traders and urban professionals, in which the weight of its agrarian bosses was greatest, and its policies reflected the interests of these groups, unconcerned with the fate of the poor. But they suffered no electoral retribution for this. Why not?

---

8   Notoriously, the end of zamindar landlordism after Independence merely transferred power in the countryside to rich farmers, the purpose for which Congress legislation was designed. For a telling case study, see Peter Reeves, 'The Congress and the Abolition of Zamindari in Uttar Pradesh', in Masselos (ed) *Struggling and Ruling: The Indian National Congress, 1885–1985*, pp. 154–167.

9   Spending on education actually fell as proportion of the budget between the First and Second Five-Year Plans: Judith Brown, *Nehru: A Political Life*, p. 236.

The answer lay, and has always lain, in what has also set India apart from any other country in the world, the historic peculiarities of its system of social stratification. Structurally, by reason of their smaller numbers and greater resources, virtually all ruling classes enjoy an advantage over the ruled in their capacity for collective action. Their internal lines of communication are more compact; their wealth offers an all-purpose medium of power, convertible into any number of forms of domination; their intelligence systems scan the political landscape from a greater height. More numerous and more dispersed, less equipped materially, less armed culturally, sub-ordinate classes always tend, in the sociologist Michael Mann's phrase, to be 'organizationally outflanked' by those above them. Nowhere has this condition been more extreme than in India. There the country is divided into some thirty major linguistic groups, under the cornice of the colonial language – the only one in which rulings on the Constitution are accessible – of which, at most, a tenth of the population has any command. These would be obstacles in themselves daunting enough to any national coordination of the poor.

But the truly deep impediments to collective action, even within language communities, let alone across them, lay in the impassible trenches of the caste system. Hereditary, hierarchical, occupational, striated through and through with phobias and taboos, Hindu social organization fissured the population into some five thousand *jati*s, few with any uniform status or definition across the country. No other system of inequality, dividing not simply, as in most cases, noble from commoner, rich from the poor, trader from farmer, learned from unlet-tered, but the clean from the unclean, the seeable from the unseeable, the wretched from the abject, the abject from the subhuman, has ever been so extreme, and so hard-wired with religious force into human expectation. The role of caste in the political system would change, from the years after independence to the present. What would not change was its structural significance as the ultimate secret of Indian democracy. Gandhi declared that caste alone had preserved Hinduism from disintegration. His judgement can be given a more contemporary application. Caste is what preserved Hindu democracy from disintegration. Fixing in hierarchical position and dividing from each other every disadvantaged group, legitimating every misery in this life as a penalty for moral transgression in a previous incarnation, it struck away any possibility of broad collective action to redress earthly injustice that might otherwise have threatened the stability of the parliamentary order over which Congress serenely presided for two decades after independence, as it became the habitual framework of the nation. Winding up the debate in the Constituent Assembly that approved the Constitution, of which he was a leading architect, Ambedkar famously remarked: 'We are going to enter a life of contradictions. In politics, we will have equality and in social and economic life, we will have inequality… We must remove this contradiction at the earliest possible moment or else those who suffer from inequality will blow up the structure of political democracy which this assembly has so laboriously constructed'. He underestimated the system of inequality against which he had fought for so long. It was not a contradiction of the democracy to come. It was the condition of it. India would be a caste-iron democracy.

What of the second great claim for which the Constitution could legitimately be held to lay the basis, the resilient unity achieved in a country of such immense diversity? Its drafters studiously avoided the word 'federal'. The Upper House in Delhi would be not even the weak shadow of a Senate. The new state would be an Indian Union, with powers conferred on the centre to manipulate or overthrow elected authorities in its constituent units unthinkable in the United States, Canada, Australia or other models consulted in its construction. But though less than federal in intention, in outcome the Union became something like a creatively flexible federation, in which state governments came to enjoy a considerable degree of autonomy, so long as they not did offer opportunities for intervention by internal disputes, or cross too boldly the political will of the centre. The test of this undeclared federalism came with the emergence of movements for linguistic redivision of territorial units inherited from the Raj. The Congress High Command was instinctively hostile to these, Nehru particularly dismissive. But popular pressures in the Telugu zone of the Madras Presidency eventually forced Delhi to accept the creation of Andhra in 1953. Top-down reorganization brought Karnataka, Kerala and Madhya Pradesh into being three years later, and after considerable violence, the Bombay Presidency had to be split into Maharashtra and Gujarat in 1960.

Thereafter the principle that if there was strong regional demand for them, new states could emerge on a linguistic or other basis was effectively conceded. At Independence there were fourteen states in the Union; today they number twenty-eight and still counting, with proposals to split UP into four states now on the agenda. In no case have voters as such ever been consulted in these redivisions: the centre has broken up states, reactively or preemptively, according to its own judgement of what exigencies required. Yet the institutional evolution that has permitted this multiplicity of regional governments to take shape must be accounted the most distinctive achievement of the Indian Constitution. That so many linguistic divisions could coexist in a single huge polity without generating insuperable disputes or deadlocks has certainly also been due to the luck of the cultural draw itself. Had either one language-group constituted a clear majority of the nation, or none enjoyed any particular preponderance over any other, the potential for conflict or scission would have been much greater. Hindi, whose native-speakers comprise some 40 per cent of the population, had just the right weight to act as a ballast in the political system, without risk of too provocatively lording over it. Still, that the contours of a mobile federalism could develop so constructively is owed to the good sense of those who redrew the map of India, originally against the wishes of Congress.

This real achievement has, in what by now could be termed the Indian Ideology, been surcharged with claims to a largely imaginary status – the notion that the preservation by the Indian state of the unity of the country is a feat so unique as to be little short of a miracle, in the standard phrase. There is no basis for this particular vanity. A glance at the map of the post-colonial world is enough to show that, no matter how heterogeneous or artificial the boundaries of any given European colony may have been, they continue to exist today. Of the fifty-two countries in Africa, the vast majority of them utterly arbitrary fabrications of rival imperialist powers, just one – Sudan – has failed to persist within the same frontiers as an independent state. In Asia, the same pattern has held, the separation of Singapore from Malaysia after two years of cohabitation not even a break with the colonial past, of Bangladesh from Pakistan enabled by external invasion. Such few sports of history aside, the motto of independence has invariably been:

what empire has joined, let no man put asunder. In this general landscape, India represents not an exception, but the rule.

That rule has, in one state after another, been enforced with violence. In Africa, wars in Nigeria, Mali, the Western Sahara, Ethiopia, Congo, Angola; in South-East Asia, the Philippines, Indonesia, Burma, Sri Lanka. Typically, military force deployed to preserve post-colonial unity has meant military government in one guise or another in society at large: state of emergency in the periphery, dictatorship at the centre. India has escaped the latter. But it has exhibited the former, with a vengeance. It is now sixty-five years since Congress seized the larger part of Kashmir, without title from the colonial power, though with vice-regal connivance, in the name of a forged document of accession from its feudal ruler, the assent of its leading politician, and the pledge of a plebiscite to confirm the will of its people. Having secured the region, Nehru – the prime mover – made short work of all three. The maharajah was soon deposed, the promise of a referendum ditched. What of the politician, on whom now rested what claims of legitimacy for Indian possession remained?

Abdullah, the 'Lion of Kashmir' as he enjoyed being styled, was a Muslim leader who, like Badshah Khan in the North-West Frontier Province, been an ally of Congress in the years of struggle against the Raj, and become the most prominent opponent of the Maharajah in the Valley of Kashmir. There his party, the National Conference, had adopted a secular platform in which local Communists had played some role, seeking independence for Kashmir as the 'Switzerland of Asia'. But when Partition came, Abdullah made no case of this demand. For some years he had bonded emotionally with Nehru, and when fighting broke out in Kashmir in the autumn of 1947, he was flown out from Srinagar to Delhi by military aircraft and lodged in Nehru's house, where he took part in planning the Indian take-over, to which he was essential. Two days later, the Maharajah – now safely repaired to Jammu – announced in a backdated letter to Mountbatten, drafted by his Indian minders, that he would install Abdullah as his Prime Minister.

For the next five years, Abdullah ruled the Valley of Kashmir and Jammu under the shield of the Indian Army, with no other authority than his reluctant appointment by a feudatory he despised and Delhi soon discarded. At the outset, Nehru believed his friend's popularity capable of carrying all before it. When subsequent intelligence indicated other-wise, talk of a plebiscite to ratify it ceased. Abdullah enjoyed genuine support in his domain, but how wide it was, or how deep, was not something Congress was prepared to bank on. Nor, it soon became clear, was Abdullah himself willing to put it to the test. No doubt acutely aware that Badshah Khan, with a much stronger popular base than himself, had lost just such a referendum in the North-West Frontier Province, he rejected any idea of one. No elections were held until 1951, when voters were finally summoned to the polls for a Constituent Assembly. Less than 5 per cent of the nominal electorate cast a ballot, but otherwise the results could not have been improved in Paraguay or Bulgaria. The National Conference and its clients won all 75 seats – 73 of them without even a contest.[10] A year later Abdullah announced the end of the Dogra dynasty and an agreement with Nehru reserving special rights for Kashmir and Jammu, limiting the powers of the Centre, within the Indian Union. But no Constitution emerged, and not even

---

10   Alastair Lamb, *Kashmir: A Disputed Legacy 1846–1990*, Hertingfordbury 1991, p. 192

the Maharajah's son, Regent since 1949, was removed, instead simply becoming Head of State.

By now, however, Delhi was becoming uneasy at the regime it had set up in Srinagar. In power, Abdullah's main achievement had been an agrarian reform putting Congress's record of inaction on the land to shame. But its political condition of possibility was confessional: the landlords expropriated were Hindu, the peasants who benefited Muslim. The National Conference could proclaim itself secular, but its policies on the land and in government employment catered to the interests of its base, which had always been in Muslim-majority areas, above all the Valley of Kashmir. Jammu, which after ethnic cleansing by Dogra forces in 1947 now had a Hindu majority, was on the receiving end of Abdullah's system, subject to an unfamiliar repression. Enraged by this reversal, the newly founded Jana Sangh in India joined forces with the local Hindu party, the Praja Parishad, in a violent campaign against Abdullah, charged with heading not only a communal Muslim, but a communist regime in Srinagar. In the summer of 1953, the Indian leader of this agitation, S.P. Mookerjee, was arrested crossing the border into Jammu, and promptly expired in a Kashmiri jail.

This was too much for Delhi. Mookerjee had, after all, been Nehru's confederate in not dissimilar Hindu agitation to lock down the partition of Bengal, rewarded with a Cabinet post, and though since then an opponent of the Congress regime, was still a member in reasonably good standing of the Indian political establishment. Abdullah, moreover, was now suspected of recidivist hankering for an independent Kashmir. The Intelligence Bureau had little difficulty convincing Nehru that he had become a liability, and overnight he was dismissed

by the stripling heir to the Dogra throne he had so complacently made his head of state, and thrown into an Indian jail on
charges of sedition.[11] His one-time friend behind bars, Nehru
installed the next notable down in the National Conference,
Bakshi Gulam Mohammed, in his place. Brutal and corrupt,
Bakshi's regime – widely known as BBC: the Bakshi Brothers
Corporation – depended entirely on the Indian security apparatus. After ten years, in which his main achievement was to do
away with any pretense that Kashmir was other than 'an inte-
gral part of the Union of India', Bakshi's reputation had become
a liability to Delhi, and he was summarily ousted in turn, to be
replaced after a short interval by another National Conference
puppet, this time a renegade communist, G.M. Sadiq, whose
no less repressive regime proceeded to wind up the party altogether, dissolving it into Congress.

Abdullah, meanwhile, sat in an Indian prison for twelve
years, eventually on charges of treason, with two brief inter-
missions in 1958 and 1964. During the second of these, he held
talks with Nehru in Delhi and Ayub in Rawalpindi, just before
Nehru died and he was re-arrested for having had the temerity to meet Zhou Enlai in Algiers. Much sentimentality has
been expended on the lost opportunity for a better settlement

---

11 For a grimly comic account of the travails of Nehru and his police chief
as accusations of conspiracy were confected against Abdullah, see B.N.
Mullik, *My Years with Nehru: Kashmir*, New Delhi 1971, pp. 86–106,
169–174. It took five years from Abdullah's arrest in 1953 for charges
to be laid against him, and another four years before they were brought
before a court, where 'witnesses showed signs of wavering', while 'some
of our most sensitive agents had been exposed and it was difficult even
to keep them safe in the valley', until Nehru – while declaring that 'he
firmly believed the evidence adduced on court was correct' – confessed
to Mullik that 'it would be impossible to convince the people at large
about the truth of the case when it was dragging on so long', and eventually – a decade after Abdullah's imprisonment – released him.

in Kashmir, when a troubled Nehru was supposedly willing to contemplate some loosening of the Indian grip on the Valley, tragically frustrated by his death. The reality is that Nehru, having seized Kashmir by force in 1947, had rapidly discovered that Abdullah and his party were neither as popular nor as secular as he had imagined, and that he could hold his prey only by an indefinite military occupation with a façade of collaborators, each less satisfactory than the last. The ease with which the National Conference was manipulated to Indian ends, as Abdullah was discarded for Bakshi, and Bakshi for Sadiq, made it clear how relatively shallow an organization it had, despite appearances, always been. By the end of his life, Nehru would have liked a more presentable fig-leaf for Indian rule, but that he had any intention of allowing a free expression of the popular will in Kashmir can be excluded: he could never afford to do so. He had shown no compunction in incarcerating on trumped-up charges the ostensible embodiment of the ultimate legitimacy of Indian conquest of the region, and no hesitation in presiding over subcontracted tyrannies of whose nature he was well aware.[12] When an anguished admirer from Jammu pleaded with him not to do so, he replied that the national interest was more important than democracy: 'We have gambled at the international stage on Kashmir, and we cannot afford to lose. At the moment we are there at the point of a bayonet. Till things improve, democracy and morality can

---

12 For a blistering attack on attempts to distance Nehru from the imprisonment of Abdullah and successive police regimes in Kashmir – he had himself, of course, always sought to shift public responsibility for them to local agents – see A.G. Noorani, 'The Legacy of 1953', *Frontline*, 16–29 August 2008, which begins: 'A monstrous wrong demands monstrous efforts to cover it up and monstrous falsehoods to justify it to the people'. Noorani is an Advocate in the Supreme Court of India.

wait'.[13] Sixty years later the bayonets are still there, democracy nowhere in sight.

On the symmetrical wing of the Union to the east, matters were not better. There the British had conquered an area larger than UP, most of it composed of the far end of what James Scott has described the Appalachia of South-east Asia: densely forested mountainous uplands inhabited by tribal peoples of Tibeto-Mongoloid origin untouched by Hinduism, with no historical connexion to any subcontinental polity. In the valleys, three Hindu kingdoms had long existed, the oldest in Manipur, the largest in Assam. The region had lain outside the Maurya and Gupta empires, and had resisted Mughal annexation. But by the early nineteenth century, Assam had fallen to Burmese expansion, and when the British seized it from Burma, they did not reinstate its dynasty, while leaving princely rule in the the much smaller states of Manipur and Tripura in place. The spread of tea plantations and logging made Assam a valuable province of the Raj, but the colonial authorities took care to separate the tribal uplands from the valleys, demarcating large zones throughout the region with an 'Inner Line' as 'Excluded and Unadministered Areas', into which they made little effort to penetrate. So remote were these from anything to do with India, even as constituted by the Victorian Empire, that when Burma was detached from the Raj in 1935, officials came close to allocating them to Rangoon rather than Delhi.

The arrival of independence would, in its own way, make the links of the North-East to the rest of India even more tenuous than before. For once Partition came down, only a thin corridor, at its narrowest some twelve miles wide, connected it

---

13　Balraj Puri, *Kashmir Towards Insurgency*, New Delhi 1993, p. 46: 'Nehru warned me against being too idealistic and asserted that the national interest was more important than democracy'.

to the body of the Union. Just 2 per cent of its borders were now contiguous with India – 98 per cent with Burma, Bangladesh, China, Nepal, and Bhutan. Manipur had no direct road connexion to India at all. Confronted with difficulties like these, the Congress leaders did not stand on ceremony. The ruler of Manipur had not been adequately rounded up along with his fellow princes by V.P. Menon in 1947, and by 1949 was resisting full integration into the Union. Briefed on the problem, Patel had just one short question: 'Isn't there a brigadier in Shillong?'. Within days, the Maharajah was kidnapped, and surrounded by troops and cut off from the outside world, at gun point made to sign his kingdom into oblivion.[14] With it went the elected assembly of the state, which for the next decade was ruled – like Tripura, brigaded into the Union at the same time – with no pretense of popular consultation by a commissioner from Delhi.

Dispersed tribes in the uplands did not permit this kind of *coup de main*, and there trouble started even before the departure of the British. In Assam, about half the Naga population of 1.5 million – some fifteen major tribes, speaking thirty languages – had been converted to Christianity by Baptist missionaries, and acquired an educated leadership in the shape of a Naga National Council, which made clear it did not want to be empressed into any future Indian state. A month before Independence, a delegation called on Gandhi in Delhi, who told them: 'You can be independent' – characteristically adding: 'You are safe as far as India is concerned. India has shed her blood for freedom. Is she going to be deprive others of their freedom? Personally, I believe you all belong to me (*sic*), to

---

14 Sanjib Baruah, *Durable Disorder: Understanding the Politics of Northeast India*, New Delhi 2005, pp. 59–60.

India. But if you say you don't, no one can force you'.[15] Congress
was less emollient. Nehru dismissed the emergent Naga leader
Phizo as a crank, and idea of Naga independence as absurd.

Undeterred, the Naga leaders declared Independence a
day before Britain transferred power to India. Congress paid
no attention. Phizo continued to tramp villages for Naga
demands, increasing support among the tribes. In March 1952,
he met Nehru In Delhi. Beside himself at Phizo's positions,
Nehru – 'hammering the table with clenched fists' – exclaimed:
'Whether heavens fall or India goes into pieces and blood runs
red in the country, whether I am here or anyone else, Nagas will
not be allowed to be independent'.[16] A year later, accompanied
by his daughter, he arrived on an official visit as Prime Minister
at Kohima, in the centre of Naga country, in the company of
the Burmese Oremier U Nu.[17] Petitioners were brushed aside.
Whereupon, when he strode into the local stadium to address a
public meeting, the audience got up and walked out, smacking
their bottoms at him in a gesture of Naga contempt. This was an

---

15 *CWMG*, Vol 88, pp. 373–374 – 19 July 1947 [*CWMG*, Vol 96, pp. 84–85]

16 See Nirmal Nibedon, *North-East India. The Ethnic Explosion*, New Delhi
    1981, p. 25. Nibedon was a brave reporter from Assam, married to a
    Naga.

17 For an shaken account by the head of Nehru's intelligence, see B.N.
    Mullik, *My Years with Nehru 1948–1964*, New Delhi 1972, p. 305: 'This
    was probably the first time when a public meeting to be addressed by
    Pandit Nehru, the darling of India's crowds, to hear and see whom people
    would trudge scores of miles, was effectively boycotted and he was left to
    address a few dozens of Government servants and their family members,
    most of whom were not Nagas, but plains people. The Prime Minister
    was shocked. So was U Nu. We could not talk. We came back to the DC's
    house where sumptuous food awaited us, but none had any appetite'. For
    Mullick, top police bludgeon in the subsequent repression, the lesson was
    clear: 'Phizo demonstrated the hold which he had already acquired on
    the Nagas, and ths incident also demonstrated the unity of the Nagas in
    their demand for independence'.

indignity worse even than he had suffered among the Pathans. The Naga National Council was de-recognized, police raids multiplied. Underground, a Naga army assembled in the hills.

By late 1955 a Naga Federal Government had been proclaimed, and a full-scale war for independence had broken out. Under the commander-in-chief of the Indian Army, two divisions and thirty-five battalions of the paramilitary Assam Rifles, a largely Gurkha force notorious for its cruelties, were dispatched to crush the uprising. As in Malaya and Vietnam, villagers were forcibly relocated in strategic hamlets to cut off support for 'hostiles' – Indian officialese banning even use of the term 'rebels'. In 1958, Nehru's regime enacted perhaps the most sanguinary single piece of repressive legislation in the annals of liberal democracy, the Armed Forces Special Powers Regulation, which authorized the killing out of hand of anyone observed in a group of five persons or more, if such were forbidden, and forbade any legal action whatsoever against 'any person in respect of anything done or purported to be done in exercise of the powers of this regulation', unless the central government so consented.[18] With this license to murder, Indian troops and paramilitaries were guaranteed immunity from atrocities, and made ample use of it. The brutality of Delhi's

18 For the text of the Regulation, see W. Lasuh (ed), *The Naga Chronicle*, New Delhi 2002, pp. 155–157. 'Any Commissioned Officer, warrant Officer, or non-Commissioned officer not below the rank of Havildar of the armed forces may, in a disturbed area: if he is of the opinion that it is necessary to do so for the maintenance of public order, after giving such due warning as he may consider necessary, fire upon or otherwise use force, even to the causing of death, against any person who is acting in contravention of any law or order for the time being in force in the disturbed area prohibiting the assembly of five persons or more'- 'No prosecution, suit or other legal proceeding shall be instituted, except with the previous sanction of the central Government, against any person in respect of anything done or purported to be done in exercise of the powers conferred by this Regulation'.

occupation of Nagaland far exceeded that of Kashmir. But as in Srinagar, so in Kohima pacification also required the suborning of local notables to construct a compliant façade of voluntary integration, work that in Naga territory was entrusted to the Intelligence Bureau. Once assured of this, Nagaland was promoted to statehood within the Union in 1963. Half a century later, the Armed Forces Special Powers Act is still required to hold the region down.

In the mid-thirties Nehru had published a book on *The Unity of India*. As a ruler, his career began and ended with bids to enforce his conception of it. Kashmir, whose seizure was the the first major act of his tenure after independence, came to occupy more Indian diplomatic time and energy, under one who prized his role on the international stage, than any other issue. His undoing came with another territorial dispute, where he could not exercise his will so easily. 'Not a yard of India is going to go out of India', he declared in Shillong in December 1957.[19] By then, China had already completed a seven hundred mile road from Sinkiang to Tibet, passing through the uninhabited Aksai Chin plateau, claimed as part of India, without anyone in Delhi being aware of it. No part of the borderlands lying between India and China had, in fact, ever been demarcated. In the east, India took lands as its own that the Raj claimed by virtue of a convention never accepted by the fledgling Chinese Republic in 1913, but agreed at Simla in 1914 by the Tibetan authorities over whom Britain acknowledged China to be suzerain, and with and from whom Britain had undertaken by earlier agreements neither to negotiate directly nor to annex territory.

---

19 Sarvepalli Gopal, *Jawaharlal Nehru: A Biography*, Vol III, London 1984, p. 30.

Even by the standards of the Raj, the degree of chica-
nery involved in this transaction was unusual. In the words
of an American jurist: 'The documents reveal the responsible
officials of British India to have acted to the injury of China
in conscious violation of their instructions; deliberately mis-
informing their superiors in London of their actions; altering
documents whose publication had been ordered by Parliament;
lying at an international conference table; and deliberately
breaking a treaty between the United Kingdom and Russia'.[20]
The result, called after its architect, was the McMahon Line.
But the Line remained so notional, the territory it claimed so
little penetrated, that it was not until 1935 that another British
functionary in Delhi noticed that the agreement wrested from
Tibetans was not included in the British lexicon of international treaties, and official maps of India still showed the
border as traditionally claimed by China; whereupon all copies
of the lexicon were recalled for destruction, and a backdated
one was produced by the Foreign Office with a forged year
of publication. If this was the position on the eastern wing of
the Raj, juridical visibility was still less on its north-western
salient. There, in 1897 the Director of Military Intelligence in
London had urged Britain to take the whole of Aksai Chin as a
buffer against Russia. Deprecating this idea, two years later the
Viceroy proposed its division in a note to China ignored by the
Qing court. In 1913, at Simla itself, the British maps marked
all of it as belonging to China. By 1927, however, without any
other supervening change, British maps showed it as part of
India. Down to the end of the Raj, the British made no attempt
to occupy the region.

---

20 Alfred Rubin, reviewing Alastair Lamb, *The McMahon Line*, in *The
American Journal of International Law*, July 1967, p. 827.

In 1956, Zhou Enlai, pointing out to Nehru that borders between their two countries had never been agreed by any treaty in the past, and needed to be determined, told him that notwithstanding its imperialist origins, China was willing to take a 'more or less realistic position' on the McMahon Line. To this Nehru replied that the northern frontiers of the British empire, as bequeathed to India, were unnegotiable. On discovering two years later that China had built a road through Aksai Chin, he demanded it withdraw. On getting a reply that Aksai Chin was part of China, Delhi initially conceded that the area was 'a matter in dispute', then hastily reversed itself.[21] There could be no question of a dispute, and no question of negotations: the Chinese must get out. The following year, revolt broke out in Tibet, and the Dalai Lama fled to India, where the CIA had for some time been helping Tibetan rebels with Indian connivance.[22] The Dalai's arrival was of no comfort to India on the border dispute – complaining of Indian recognition of Chinese sovereignty over Tibet, he pointed out that 'If you deny sovereign status to Tibet, you deny the validity of the Simla Convention and therefore the validity of the McMahon Line'[23] – but it increased tensions between Beijing and Delhi. Nevertheless, in 1960 Zhou Enlai arrived from Rangoon, fresh from a boundary agreement accepting the McMahon line where it abutted on Burma, and proposed a similar acceptance

---

21 In 1953, the foreign secretary of the time later confessed, 'our experts had advised us that our claim to Aksai Chin was not too strong': Raghavan, *War and Peace in Modern India*, p. 240.

22 By 1963 the CIA was training Tibetan guerrillas under the direct supervision of a Sikh general in two Indian bases, one near Dehra Dun, the other in Orissa, both ceremonially inspected by Nehru before his death: see Kenneth Conboy and James Morrison, *The CIA's Secret War in Tibet*, Lawrence 2002, pp. 187, 192.

23 Neville Maxwell, *India's China War*, London 1970, p. 99.

with India, in exchange for its assent that Aksai Chin belonged to China.[24] Once again, he was told there could be no negotiations over Indian claims in their plenitude.

Legally, these rested simply on the expansionist chicaneries of the Raj in the east, and – even less – its cartographic fancies in the west. Politically, however, the reality was that on either side of the mountain chains separating the subcontinent from the plateaux to the north, both Qing and Victorian regimes were systems of imperial conquest over subject peoples. The Qing was an older presence in the region, and by what passed for the diplomatic proprieties of the time, its weak successor had been defrauded of territory by the British. The corpse of one predator had been robbed by another, with otherwise little to choose between them. Half a century later, China was a revolutionary state actuated not by legal injury but strategic utility. Aksai Chin was of use to it, whereas it was of so little significance to India it had not even noticed that China had built a road through the region. Territory south of the McMahon Line was of little use to it, and India could keep it. Had Nehru shown a grain of historical common sense, or political realism, he would have settled on that basis. Indian public opinion, it is often said, debarred this, and certainly he feared, as he told his officials, that 'If I give them that I shall no longer be Prime Minister of India – I will not do it.'[25] But, of course, no-one was more responsible for the fantasies of a sempiternal India, stretching back millenia across every yard of land claimed by

---

24   M. Taylor Fravel, *Strong Borders, Secure Nation: Cooperation and Conflict in China's Territorial Disputes*, Princeton 2008, pp. 88–94.

25   Maxwell, *India's China War*, p. 161. A leading apologist puts Nehru's position in the euphemistic jargon of contemporary punditry. Nehru had 'to assess constantly what the political marketplace would bear, and to adopt only those policies which could be sold to the public': Raghavan, *War and Peace in Modern India*, p. 253.

the Raj, than Nehru himself. This was the dream-world of the 'Unity' and 'Discovery' of India in which he had soaked himself since the thirties, and was now inspiring the surreal claim that the McMahon Line coincided with the borders of India for nearly three thousand years, in which 'the striving of the Indian spirit was directed towards these Himalayan fastnesses', as testified by the Upanishads.[26]

In the grip of delusions such as these, all contact with reality was lost. Troops were ordered to take up forward positions, challenging outposts of the PLA in Aksai Chin, and in the North East. Nehru's Chief of Staff, his Kashmiri favourite B.M. Kaul, declared that 'a few rounds fired at the Chinese would cause them to run away'. His Home Minister – and later successor – Shastri announced that if China did not vacate the disputed areas, India would eject it from them as summarily as it had Portugal from Goa. In September 1962 – Nehru himself, attending another meaningless Commonwealth conference in London, was not even in Delhi – the decision was made to do so, without the slightest idea of what might ensue. Burning villages in Nagaland and shooting demonstrators in Srinagar in the name of national unity was one thing: that the Indian Army could do. Taking on the PLA in the same cause was another matter. In a first round of fighting, lasting a fortnight in October, Indian troops attempting to advance in the North-East were thrashed, while garrisons fell in the west. The shock in Delhi was great, but did not sober Nehru, who in characteristic style thanked China during the succeeding lull for an action that has 'suddenly lifted a veil from the face of India' – in

---

26 Maxwell, *India's China War*, p. 127. The best Indian critique of Nehru's conception of the nation is to be found in Javeed Alam's outstanding essay, 'The Nation and the State in India. A Difficult Bond', *India's Living Constitution*, pp. 83–104, esp. 92–95.

full rhetorical flight, images from the boudoir were rarely far from his mind – affording 'a glimpse of the serene face of India, strong and yet calm and determined, an ancient face which is ever young and vibrant'.[27]

US, British and Israeli weapons were hastily summoned to bulk up the national arsenal. On Nehru's birthday, 14 November, his troops launched an counter-attack in the North-East. Within less than week, they were ignominiously routed, disintegrating completely as a military force. Had China wished, the PLA could have marched without opposition to Calcutta. In panic, Nehru pleaded for American bombers to attack it.[28] But the Chinese leadership had already achieved all that it intended to do, and its control of Aksai Chin now beyond challenge, withdrew its troops back across the McMahon Line in a move of olympian closure virtually as humiliating to Nehru as his crushing defeat in the field. The Caporetto of Thagla Ridge effectively finished him. Psychologically broken and physically diminished, he lingered in office for another eighteen months before his death in the spring of 1964.

In retrospect, Nehru's stock has risen among Indian intellectuals of liberal or left persuasion as that of the political class that came after him has fallen. That is understandable: he belonged to a generation that had resisted the British in the name of an ideal, with no certainty of success in their life-time, and paid for it, as those who came to power thereafter by birth or intrigue did not. But it is also a limited basis for historical

---

27 Maxwell, *India's China War*, p. 381.

28 Kaul, from a bed in Delhi, 'produced from under his pillow', a paper urging the government 'to persuade Chiang Kai-shek and also South Korean forces, assisted by the United States' potential in the West Pacific seaboard, to invade the Chinese mainland', and hoping the USAF would 'launch massive attacks on China from bases in India': Steven Hoffman, *India and the China Crisis*, Berkeley-Los Angeles 1990, p. 198.

judgement. The image of a ruler-sage was always misplaced. As those who knew and admired him at close range were well aware, he was – in the words of Sarvepalli Gopal, the loyal assistant who became his principal biographer – a 'commonplace mind' that was 'not capable of deep or original thought'.[29] The shallowness of his intellectual equipment was connected to the side of his personality that drifted so easily away from realities resistant to his hopes or fancies. It is striking how similar was the way two such opposite contemporaries as Patel and Jinnah could see him – the former speaking on occasion of his 'childlike innocence', the latter comparing him to Peter Pan.[30] Gopal's image is more telling still: early on, Nehru 'made a cradle of emotional nationalism and rocked himself in it',[31] as if a child cocooning himself to sleep from the outside world. He had, of course, many qualities that were more adult: hard work, ambition, charm, ruthlessness. With these went others that were developmentally ambiguous: sanctimony, petulance, violent outbursts of temper, vanity. Occupational hazards of high office, no doubt. Yet however self-satisfied, few politicians could write, as he did before his death, that no-one had ever been loved so much by millions of his compatriots as himself. Abstemious in many other ways, and little attracted to the supernatural, his opiate – another admirer would remark[32] – was the adoration of the people.

---

29 *Jawaharlal Nehru*, Vol II, London 1979, p. 316. *The Discovery of India* was a ' jumble of a book', full of 'woolly writing' and 'many meaningless sentences': Vol I, pp. 298–299.

30 B. Krishna, *Sardar Vallabhbhai Patel*, New Delhi 1996, p. 24; Stanley Wolpert, *Nehru. A Tryst with Destiny*, London 1966, p. 44.

31 *Jawaharlal Nehru*, Vol I, London 1975, p. 69.

32 Walter Crocker, *Nehru: A Contemporary's Estimate*, London 1966, p.153: 'Religion may or may not be the opiate of the people, but the people were the opiate of Nehru'. Crocker, a conservative diplomat who served as

The disabling effects of this addiction lacked an antidote among his colleagues. Patel, who could have counter-balanced it, was soon dead. Nehru took care to appoint no Deputy Premier to succeed him. Rajagopalachari, who had been President, went in his view 'off the rails', exiting Congress. Ambedkar, whom Nehru feared, and whose funeral he pointedly failed to attend, was rapidly edged out. Bose, the only leader Congress ever produced who united Hindus, Muslims and Sikhs in a common secular struggle, and would have most threatened him, lay buried in Taiwan: the political landscape of post-war India would not have been the same had he survived. Surrounded by mediocrities, Nehru accumulated more posts than he could handle – permanent Foreign Minister as well as Prime Minister, not to speak of Defense Minister, Head of the Planning Commission, President of Congress, at various times. He was not a good administrator, finding it difficult to delegate, but even had he been, this was a pluralism too far. In Gopal's view, government became 'a one-man show'.[33] That was not entirely just, since Nehru could not attend to everything, so a notional Cabinet also meant that Ministers could often do what they liked in their Departments as well.

The most damaging feature of the regime that crystallized around him was less this centrifugal aspect than the development of a court of sycophants at extra-ministerial level. Unlike Gandhi, Nehru was a poor judge of character, and his choice of confidantes consistently disastrous.[34] Promoting to

Australian ambassador to India for some six years between the mid fifties and early sixties, saw Nehru at close range and with great warmth. After the passage of a half century, his short book remains perhaps the most perceptive portrait of him as a man and a ruler.

33 *Jawaharlal Nehru*, Vol II, p. 304.

34 'In the circumambient mixture of sycophancy and flattery', as Crocker put it, 'more than one mountebank and not a few crooks did well out of

Chief of Staff over the heads of senior officers his henchman in overthrowing Abdullah, Brij Mohan Kaul, a poltroon from Kashmir with no battlefield experience who fled the field at the first opportunity, Nehru was directly responsible for the Indian debacle of 1962. For his personal secretary, he installed a repellent familiar from Kerala, M.O. Mathai, who acquired inordinate power, taking his master's daughter to bed and his paper-work to the CIA, until his reputation became so noxious that Nehru was reluctantly forced to part with him.[35] For political operations in Kashmir, the North-East or closer to home, he relied on a dim police thug, Bhola Nath Mullik, formerly of British employ, head of the Intelligence Bureau. The only actual colleague he really trusted was Krishna Menon, an incompetent windbag who ended in disgrace along with Kaul.

Still, it can be argued that such failings were trifling set beside one commanding achievement. Nehru's greatness, it is generally felt, was to rule as a democrat in a non-Western world teeming with dictators. Preceptor to his nation, he set an example from which those who came after him could not long depart. Tutored by him, Indian democracy found its feet, and has lasted ever since. That by conviction Nehru was a liberal democrat is clear. Nor was this a merely theoretical attachment to principles of parliamentary government. As Prime Minister, Nehru took his duties in the Lok Sabha with a conscientious punctilio putting many a Western ruler to shame, regularly speaking and debating in the chamber, and never

---

his aberrations of judgement': *Nehru*, pp. 86, 140.

35 Gopal, *Jawaharlal Nehru*, Vol II, p. 122, Vol III, pp. 310–312; for Mathai's own version of himself, see *Reminiscences of the Nehru Age*, New Delhi 1978. Its notorious blank chapter 'She', recounting 'without inhibition in the D.H. Lawrence style' his affair with Nehru's daughter, was circulated privately.

resorted to rigging national elections, or suppressing a wide range of opinion. So much is incontestable. But liberalism is a metal that rarely comes unalloyed. Nehru was first and foremost an Indian nationalist, and where the popular will failed to coincide with the nation as he imagined it, he suppressed it without remorse. There, the instruments of government were not ballots but, as he himself blurted, bayonets.

Nor, within the zone where the nation was not contested, could democracy simply be left to its own devices. No figure was more powerful in Nehru's court than Mullik, picked for the job from Bihar by Patel, who ingratiated himself with Nehru by supplying surveillance of all opposition parties from a network of informers inside them.[36] Like other elected rulers – Nixon comes to mind – Nehru was fascinated by such clandestine information, and came to rely on Mullik in handling Kashmir, where he became the minder of successive puppet regimes,[37] and in pressing forward on the Sino-Indian border, his counsel disastrous in both areas. But it was closer to home that his services were most critical. As Mullik's memoirs show, when a Communist government was elected in Kerala – 'always a matter of special interest to the IB' – and the local Congress

36 Not, of course, he unctuously assured Nehru, Congress itself. During regular nocturnal meetings with Nehru, Mullik recounts, 'I used to drink deep at his feet. On these occasions he appeared to me like a sage from the Upanishads explaining the Truth as realised by him to a disciple'. Nehru, who told him Genghis Khan should be the inspiration for India's intelligence service, 'had no hesitation in trusting me completely and often told me of his differences with his colleagues in the Cabinet or in Congress': *My Years with Nehru*, pp. 58, 61–2, 66.

37 For the closeness with which Mullik monitored and micro-managed the scene in Kashmir, see his boast that from 1952 onwards: 'At every crisis in Kashmir's history, I used to be personally present in Kashmir and work shoulder to shoulder with the Kashmir leaders to surmount their difficulties: *My Years with Nehru*, p. 32.

establishment connived at religious agitation to overthrow it, the Intelligence Bureau was central to the operation that finally brought it down, when Nehru gave the order to eliminate a democratic obstacle to will of the Centre.[38]

Such episodes have generally been portrayed as inconsistencies on Nehru's part, of a secondary kind it would not be difficult to find in the career of many another well-regarded liberal statesman. There is reason to that. The larger truth, however, is that Nehru could be the democratic ruler he was because once in office he faced so little opposition. Throughout his years as Prime Minister, Congress enjoyed enormous majorities in Parliament, and controlled virtually every provincial government, in a caste-divided society. All non-Congress governments were given their cards. [39] Given the ease of that monopoly of power – political scientists would dub it a 'one-party democracy' – there was no occasion to resort to the conventional forms of authoritarian rule. Subjectively, any prospect of a dictatorship was alien to Nehru. But objectively, it was also quite unnecessary, so little temptation ever arose. By and large, democracy across most of the Union was costless. That he handed it on as well as he did remains, nevertheless, his positive legacy.

What of the other side of the ledger? 'As Calais was written on Queen Mary's heart', Nehru told a British general in a

---

38 *My Years with Nehru*, pp. 337–367: 'Whether the Central Government's action in Kerala was constitutional and proper is now purely an academic issue', p. 357.

39 'It is a sad comment on the working of the Nehru regime that none of the non-Congress state governments escaped falling victim to the monopolistic character of the Congress party': Bhagwan Dua, 'Indian Congress Dominance Revisited', in Paul Brass and Francis Robinson (eds), *The Indian National Congress and Indian Society 1885–1985*, New Delhi, 1987, p. 359.

revealing comparison, 'so Kashmir is written on mine'. [40]. The consequences, down the decades, would be bloodier even than her reign. The inheritance he left in the North-East was much the same. In 1961, he made it a crime to question the territorial integrity of India in writing or in speech, in sign or image, punishable with three years imprisonment. The Nagas, whom he started to bomb in 1963, were unbeaten when he died. Three years later, a full-scale rebellion broke out among the neighboring Mizo. By the end of the following decade, Manipur, Tripura and Assam were all in flames. The criminality – murder, torture, rape – covered by AFSPA multiplied. Repression, cooption and exhaustion have yet to bring any real peace to the region, where India still has so much to hide that outsiders need special permission to enter, and can only visit parts of it, under strict controls. Tibet is generally easier of access to foreigners.

For the rest of the Union, the lasting affliction of Nehru's rule has been the dynastic system he left it. He claimed to reject any hereditary principle, and his capacity for self-deception was perhaps great enough for him to believe he was doing so. But his refusal to indicate any colleague as a successor, and complaisance in the elevation of his daughter – with no qualifications other than birth for the post – to the Presidency of Congress, where Gandhi had once placed him for his own trampolin to power, speak for themselves. From the outset, she was more authoritarian than her father – within weeks, her first action was to call for the ouster of the government of Kerala. Once in command of the state and not just of the party, she would in due course declare an Emergency, arresting the leaders of every

---

40 See Patrick French, *Liberty or Death: India's Journey to Independence and Division*, London 1997, p. 372.

opposition party and jailing 140,000 citizens without charges. To many, it seemed that India was on the brink of dictatorship.

In fact what had happened was an exercise, on a much larger scale than ever before, of a traditional instrument of British rule, dubbed by one of its officials with the oxymoron 'civil martial law': mass arrests, suspension of ordinary legal procedures, followed – when danger of refractory opposition was thought past – by release of prisoners and reversion to standard juridical and electoral norms.[41] This was the technique the Raj had applied to Civil Disobedience in 1932, again in 1940, and was used to bring Kerala to heel in 1959. Thereafter, in the shape of impositions of Presidential Rule, it became the Centre's regular method for disposing of state governments unsatisfactory to it, by 1977 employed no less than forty times, only five states not having subjected to it. But it could also be deployed less formally on a national scale, as when Delhi interned and deported thousands of Indian citizens of Chinese origin as enemy aliens, and arrested all Communist leaders out of hand – including even those who had rallied to the patriotic banner – during the Sino-Indian War. The difference between resort to civil martial law by father and daughter was one of degree rather than kind. After twenty months, Indira Gandhi lifted the Emergency and held elections, as the guide-book of the Raj laid down.

The Emergency was nevertheless a watershed in Indian politics, since popular reaction against it broke for the first time the monopoly of government in Delhi enjoyed by Congress since independence. The heteroclite coalition that replaced it in the elections of 1977 did not last long, and the dynasty – daughter,

---

41 For a striking analysis of this pattern, see D.A. Low, 'Emergencies and Elections in India', in his *Eclipse of Empire*, Cambridge 1991, pp. 159–163.

succeeded by grandson – was soon back at the helm. But out of the magma of post-Emergency opposition eventually emerged a party of comparable electoral strength, which two decades later was capable of forming governments as stable or unstable as those of Congress. With the arrival of the BJP in power, formally committed to the idea of Hindutva, it was less democracy which looked under threat – at least immediately; if ultimately it too, in the eyes of many – than the third value of the Indian state, its secularity.

In the struggle for independence, the legitimating ideology of Congress had always been a secular nationalism. It was in the name of that ideal it claimed to speak for the whole subcontinent, regardless of faith. Partition had divided the Raj, the Muslim League creating a state founded on Islam in Pakistan. In the run-up to Partition, British officials regularly referred to the larger area where Congress would rule as Hindustan, a term in private not always shunned by Congress leaders themselves. But when an independent state came into being, it was proudly just India, repudiating any official religious identity, proclaiming the unity of a nation that had been artificially divided. The Constitution it adopted did not, however, describe India as a secular state, a term that was avoided. Nor did it institute equality before the law, a principle also eschewed. There would be no uniform civil code: Hindus and Muslims would continue to be subject to the respective customs of their faith governing family life. Nor would there be interference with religious hierarchies in daily life: untouchability was banned, but caste itself left untouched. Protection of cows and prohibition of alcohol were enjoined, and seats reserved in Parliament for two minorities, Scheduled Castes and Tribes – Dalits and Adivasis in today's terminology – but not Muslims.

Ambedkar, responsible for much of the Constitution, was not satisfied with the upshot, and as Minister for Law introduced in 1951 a Hindu Code Bill striking down the grosser forms of marital inequality it had sanctioned. Faced with uproar from the benches of Congress – he had the temerity to tell its MPs that the cherished legend of Krishna and Radha was an emblem of Hindu degradation of women – he was unceremoniously abandoned by Nehru and the Bill neutered.[42] With his exit went the only outspoken adversary of Hindu ascendancy at large ever to serve in an Indian Cabinet. In 1947, he had been inducted into it by Patel and Nehru *à contre-coeur*, because they feared the alliance between his party, the Scheduled Castes' Federation, and Jinnah's, which had actually elected him from Bengal to the Constituent Assembly – the combination of Untouchables and Muslims that Gandhi had dreaded in the thirties. In his speech of resignation, Ambedkar made it clear he had been cold-shouldered by Nehru from the outset, who had refused to give him any post of substance in the Cabinet, and that he not only regarded the ditching of the Hindu Code Bill as a betrayal – he called it 'mental torture', but the grabbing of Kashmir and ensuing allocation of over half the budget to the Army, as unacceptable.

Nor did he feel the position of his own people had altered much meanwhile: 'the same old tyranny, the same old oppression, the same old discrimination which existed before, exists now, and perhaps in a worse form'.[43] He had reason to say that,

---

42 After Ambedkar had gone, revisions to Hindu marriage, inheritance and family law were passed in dribs and drabs between 1955 and 1956: how far he would have been satisfied with the result may be doubted. To this day, no Uniform Civil Code, and so no full equality before the law, exists in India.

43 Ambedkar, *Writing and Speeches*, Vol 14, Part Two, Bombay 1995, pp. 1318–1322.

since he had been forced to scrap even the minimal safeguards for their political autonomy conceded in the thirties, consigning their fate to Uncle Toms like the notoriously venal Jagjivan Ram, Union Minister and Untouchable pillar of Congress in UP, who made no secret of the fact that 'since one had to depend on the non-Scheduled Caste vote, one went along with the fortunes of the party.[44] Nor was Ambedkar consoled by sanctimonious plaudits for his role in drafting the Constitution. He knew he had been used by Congress, and said two years later: 'People always keep on saying to me: oh sir, you are the maker of the Constitution. My answer is, I was a hack. What I was asked to do, I did much against my will'. When his *Riddles of Hinduism* was published thirty years later, long after his death, not a Congressional whisper was heard in defence of him, amid the bigoted outcry.

Congress had failed to avert Partition because it could never bring itself honestly to confront its composition as an overwhelmingly Hindu party, and accept the need for generous arrangements with the Muslim party that had emerged opposite it, dropping the fiction that it represented the entire nation. After independence, it presided over a state which could not but bear the marks of that denial. Compared with the fate of Pakistan after the death of Jinnah, India was fortunate. If the state was not truly secular – within a couple of years, it was rebuilding with much pomp the famous Hindu temple in Somnath, ravaged by Muslim invaders, and authorizing the installation of Hindu idols in the famous mosque at Ayodhya – nor was it overtly confessional. Muslims or Christians could practice their religion with greater freedom, and live with

---

44 For these statements, see Rajeev Bhargava (ed), *Politics and Ethics of the Indian Constitution*, New Delhi 2008, pp. 255 and 119.

greater safety, than Muslims themselves would be able to do in Pakistan, if they were not Sunni. Structurally, the secularism of Congress had been a matter not of hypocrisy, but of bad faith, which is not the same: in its way a lesser vice, paying somewhat more tribute to virtue.

Around it, however, there inevitably developed a discourse to close the gap between official creed and unofficial practice, that has come to form a department of its own within the Indian Ideology. Secularism in India, it is explained, does not mean anything so unsophisticated as the separation of state and religion. Rather – so one version goes – the Indian state is secular because, while it may well finance or sponsor this or that religious institution or activity, in doing so it maintains an 'equidistance' from the variegated faiths before it.[45] For another version, this is too limitative. The state should, and does, keep a 'principled distance' from the different religions of India, but the principle is one of 'group-sensitive' flexibility, allowing both for direct – supporting or restraining – involvement in religious matters, and for non-involvement where that is the better course, without any necessary commitment to symmetry of action towards sensitive groups in either case.[46] The outcome is a richer and more rewarding texture of relations between public authorities and devout communities, more in keeping with the highest ideals of a multicultural age, than any *laicité* to be found in the West or Far East.

A leading test of these professions is the condition of the community that Congress always claimed also to represent, and

---

45 Amartya Sen, 'Secularism and Its Discontents', in *The Argumentative Indian*, London 2005, pp. 295–296 et seq.

46 Rajeev Bhargava, 'India's Secular Constitution', in Achin Vanaik and Rajeev Bhargava, *Understanding Contemporary India: Critical Perspectives*, New Delhi 2010, pp. 41–42.

the Indian state to acquit it of any shadow of confessionalism. How have Muslims fared under such secularism, equidistant or group-sensitive? In 2006, the government-appointed Sachar Commission found that of the 138 million Muslims in India, numbering some 13.4 per cent of the population, less than three out of five were literate, and one out of three were among the most destitute layers of Indian society. A quarter of their children between the ages of 6 and 14 were not in school. In the top fifty colleges of the land, two out of a hundred post-graduates were Muslim; in the elite Institutes of Technology, four out of a hundred. In the cities, Muslims had fewer chances of any regular job than Dalits or Adivasis, and higher rates of unemployment. The Indian state itself, presiding over this scene? In central government, the Report confessed, 'Muslims' shares in employment in various departments are abysmally low at all levels'–not more than 5 per cent at even the humblest rung. In state governments, the situation could be still worse – nowhere more so than in Communist-run West Bengal, which with a Muslim population of 25 per cent, nearly double the official average for the nation, many confined in ghettos of appalling misery, posted a figure of just 3.25 per cent of Muslims in its service.[47] It is possible, moreover, that the official number of Muslims in India is an underestimate. In a confidential cable to Washington released by Wikileaks, the US Embassy reported that the real figure was somewhere between 160 and 180 million.[48] Were that so, Sachar's findings would need to be deflated.

---

47 Government of India, *Social, Economic and Educational Status of the Muslim Community in India. A Report*, New Delhi 2006, pp. 52–58, 68–69, 93, 167, 367–368. Sympathizers with the CPM have contested the Report's estimates for West Bengal.

48 *Times of India*, 4 September 2011.

At Partition, most middle-class Muslims in Hindu-majority areas had emigrated to Pakistan, leaving a decapitated community of poorer co-religionaries behind. The great mass of those who remained in India thus started out from a very disadvantaged position. But what is plain is that the Indian state which now claimed to cast an impartial mantle over them did no such thing. Its discrimination against them began with the Constitution itself, which accorded rights of representation to minorities it denied to them. Scheduled Castes – Untouchables – and Scheduled Tribes were granted special constituencies and seats in the Lok Sabha, subsequently also reservations in public employment, and in due course still more Hindu groups – 'Other Backward Classes' (sc. Castes) – acquired the latter too. But Muslims were refused both, on the grounds that conceding them would violate the precepts of secularism by introducing religion into matters of state. They were thereby denied any possibility of acting collectively to better their lot. If a Muslim party had possessed any proportionate share of national representation, its interests could never have been ignored in the coalition politics that has been the norm once Congress lost its monopoly of power. To add insult to injury, even where Muslims were locally concentrated in sufficient numbers to make an electoral difference, these were not infrequently constituencies reserved for castes supposedly worse, but actually better off, than they. In mechanics such as these, Indian secularism is Hindu confessionalism by another name.

If matters are like this in the Indian state's machinery of representation, it may be imagined how they stand in its now immense apparatus of repression. All told, the 'security agencies' of the Indian Union, as the Sachar Report politely calls them, number close to two million. How many Muslims do they contain? The answer is too sensitive to divulge: as the Report notes, no figures are available for three quarters of these. Put simply, Muslims are not wanted – in their ranks, the fewer the better. In 1999, a former Defence Minister let slip that they numbered just 1 per cent out of 1,100,000 regulars. In the Research and Analysis Wing (RAW) and Intelligence Bureau (IB) – the CIA and FBI of the Indian State – it is an 'unwritten code' that there should be not a single Muslim; so too in the National Security Guards and Special Protection Group, its Secret Service corps. The Indian armed forces at large are a Hindu preserve, garnished with Sikhs, and bolstered still – a unique arrangement in the post-colonial world – by Gurkhas from Nepal, as under the Raj.[49] Mercenaries they may be, but their battle-cry could not be more impeccably Hindu: yells of 'O Goddess Kali' as they unsheath their *khukhri*.

As with other oppressed minorities in societies keen to advertise their pluralism, a sprinkling of celebrities – a batsman or film-star here, a scientist or symbolic office-holder there – adorns, but does not materially alter, the position of the overwhelming majority of Muslims in India. Unlike blacks

---

49 For particulars, see Omar Khalidi, 'Ethnic Group Recruitment in the Indian Army: the Contrasting Cases of Sikhs, Muslims, Gurkhas and Others', *Pacific Affairs*, Winter 2001–2002, pp. 529–552, and his *Khaki and the Ethnic Violence in India*, New Delhi 2003, pp. 23–24, 61–65. Sikhs, who comprise about 2.5 per cent of the population and 20 per cent of the officer corps of the army, are a far more privileged group in India than Muslims, and occupy an ambiguous position in the dispositions of the state. Against Sikh religious insurgency in Punjab, the full weight of armoured repression was unleashed; at the same time, army and air force recruitment have throughout drawn deep from the traditions of Sikh militarism. The condition of this ambiguity is the nature of the Sikh creed itself, a split-off from Hinduism, rather than a faith entirely alien to it. No objection was raised by Savarkar or the Mahasabha to Ambedkar if he wanted Dalits to become Sikhs, but Christians or Buddhists were another matter.

in the US, who comprise a roughly similar proportion of the population, they suffer from no racial stigma, and are overlaid with a thin elite layer of upper class origin, the small residue of those who did not leave for Pakistan in 1947, bearers in some degree of a historical memory of Muslim rule, without any counterpart in the descendants of slavery in America. But otherwise most Muslims in India are much worse off, because they benefit from no affirmative action, and in a caste society are perforce more endogamous. They are second-class citizens.

Their fate shows into sharp relief unspoken realities of the Indian polity that emerged after Partition, which take still more ominous form where it is contested. In such zones, the young Indian historian Ananya Vajpeyi has written, 'what the AFSPA effectively does' is 'to create an entirely separate space within India, a sort of second and shadow nation, that functions as a military state rather than an electoral democracy, and only remains hidden because it is not, at least so far, officially ruled by a general or a dictator' – a space which should 'not be thought of as a zone of exception, but as a contradiction so extreme that it undoes the totality in which it is embedded', which breaks down into 'two distinct and mutually opposed regimes' that form 'two nations: India and non-India'.[50] The description is powerful, but it looks away from the connexion between them. For what is perfectly obvious, but never seen or spoken, is that the hand of AFSPA has fallen where the reach of Hinduism has stopped. The three great insurgencies against the Indian state have come in Kashmir, Nagaland-Mizoram, and Punjab – regions respectively Muslim, Christian and Sikh. There it met popular feeling with tank and truncheon, pogrom

---

50 'Resenting the Indian State: For a New Political Practice in the North-East', in Sanjib Baruah (ed), *Beyond Counter-Insurgency. Breaking the Impasse in Northeast India*, New Delhi 2009, p. 36.

and death squad. Today, the same configuration threatens to hold true of 'the greatest danger to Indian democracy', as the current Prime Minister has called it, the Naxalite corridor that runs from Jharkhand to Andhra Pradesh: pre-Aryan tribal populations with their own forest cults, subject to ever more ruthless despoliation in their homelands. Vajpeyi's formulation is better reversed. The 'shadow nation' is not where democracy is denied, but where it is practised. What is hidden within India is Hindustan. It is that which tacitly shapes the state and determines the frontiers between freedom and repression, what is allowed and what is forbidden.[51]

Official secularity is not meaningless. If India is a confessional state, it is by default, not prescription. There is no need to be a Hindu in any sense other than by birth to be successful in bureaucratic career terms. Descent, not piety, is the criterion. Thus much of the state apparatus, especially its upper echelons, may be composed of individuals largely or entirely secular in outlook, practising or devout Hindus perhaps only a minority. Compared with the state, society is less secular. To

---

51 Hindustan: originally a Persian coinage of geographical reference, derived from the river Indus, of no particular religious connotation, transformed into a sectarian slogan as 'Hindusthan' by the Sangh. Distinct from either of these, the usage here is that of common currency in the years before Independence, when it referred to the state that would arise where Hindus were the majority, if the Raj split along religious lines, as it eventually did: for examples, see pp. 68–69 above. So far as its contemporary application is concerned, the Indian state is ruthless enough in putting down any popular resistance to it, of whatever composition, as the methods it employed to crush the first Naxalite movement showed. But it did not require AFSPA for that purpose, and the toll of killed and tortured does not compare with that in Kashmir, Nagaland or Punjab. It is where political resistance has acquired a mass character because it is informed by another religious identity that the full weight of repression has come down, and in doing so made pointedly clear the core faith demarcating, from its inception, the state itself.

that extent, the ideology of Indian secularism is grounded in a real difference, and makes a difference. An ideology it nevertheless remains. For what the character of the Indian state essentially reproduces is that of Congress as a nationalist party. It is not overtly confessional, on the contrary making much of its secular ideals, but in both composition and practice is based squarely on the Hindu community, and just as Congress made no serious effort to register or come to terms politically with the Muslim League, so the state over which the party has presided has never made any serious effort to improve the social or political position of its Muslim minority. Had the party or state been truly secular, in each case this would have been a priority, but was the last thing it had in mind. There cannot be a genuinely secular party or state unless it is willing to confront religious superstition and bigotry, rather than truckle to them. Neither party nor state has ever contemplated doing that, because both have rested, sociologically speaking, on Hindu caste society. The continued dominance of upper castes in public institutions – administration, police, courts, universities, media – belongs to the same matrix.

In the history of twentieth-century nationalism, there is a distinct sub-group in which religion played a central organizing role from the start, providing so to speak the genetic code of the movement. The most significant cases are those which eventually founded stable parliamentary democracies. The three leading states of this type in the world today are Ireland, Israel and India. In all three, the nationalist party that came to power after independence – Fine Gael, Mapai, Congress – distanced itself from the confessional undertow of the struggle; without, however, ever being able to tackle its legacy head-on. In each case, as the ruling party gradually lost its lustre, it was outflanked by a more extreme rival that had fewer inhibitions about appealing directly to the theological passions aroused by the original struggle – Fianna Fail, Likud, BJP. The success of these parties was due not just to the faltering of the first wave of office-holders, but to their ability to articulate openly what had always been latent in the national movement, but neither candidly acknowledged, nor consistently repudiated. They could claim, with a certain justice, to be legitimate heirs of the original cause. In each case, the setting was a parliamentary system, in which they operated constitutionally, if in each case with certain pre-war sympathies for European fascism: the cases of Jabotinsky and the RSS were particularly striking.

The institutional Catholicism of De Valera's Ireland, and constitutional Judaism of the Zionist state set up by Ben Gurion, were not repeated in India, where the state has never professed any such explicit religious allegiance. Historically, no Congress leader had been capable of openly and vigorously combatting Gandhian pietism, all persuaded that it offered a short-cut to independence with an emotional awakening against the British. After Independence, Gandhi's own docrines were consigned to the museum, but his saturation of politics with Hindu pathos lived on. For two generations, as in Israel, the compromised origins of the state could be masked by the charisma of a ruler who cared little for superstition of any kind, but a good deal about state-led economic development. After he went – full Hindu funeral rites on the Ganges – there was a rapid degeneration. Arguably, Nehru left a worse legacy in this respect than Ben Gurion, since he injected a further irrationalist element into the political system, blood rather than faith, with the creation of a hereditary dynasty that has been an additional curse that lingers without end. The daughter, characteristically, made more of a show of secularism, writing a belated commitment to it for the first time into the constitution, while in practice toying instrumentally with confessional appeals. By the time the grandson was in charge, the global turn to neo-liberalism in the West was in full swing, and the Indian middle class eager for its pickings. In these conditions, the ground was prepared for the BJP to enter, Likud-style, into its inheritance. In all three countries, the political system would come to rest on a more or less regular alternation between two large kindred forces, each bidding for alliance with an array of opportunist smaller parties to form majorities difficult for them to achieve by themselves – the pattern shared in the Dail, the Knesset and the Lok Sabha. In all three, the marginalization of the Left has been a structural effect of the dominance of the hegemonic religion in the national identity.

The temporalities and outcomes of the process differed. The Irish reversion came within a decade of independence: its carrier was the genuinely more popular and radical wing of the national movement, with greatest anti-colonial legitimacy from the start, and enjoyed the longest ascendancy, only finally collapsing last year. It took thirty years for the Israeli to gain the upper hand, which it still enjoys. The Indian was slower still: half a century passed before the BJP gained office. A mutation of the Hindu Mahasabha, with which Gandhi had been on good terms, it had played a very modest role in the independence struggle, coming to the fore only during Partition, when it led the campaign to divide Bengal along religious lines, pulling Congress in along with it. In the RSS, the party had a disciplined mass oranization behind it, but no fighting credentials comparable to the IRA or the Irgun. It took successive stages in the decay of Congress – the Emergency; the manipulation and repression of Sikh insurgency in Punjab; its retribution in the death of Indira Gandhi; the ensuing pogrom in Delhi, applauded by her son; the ballooning corruption around Rajiv Gandhi, and its generalization with the neo-liberal turn under Narasimha Rao – for the BJP to achieve final take-off as a credible alternative to the ruling party. But by the nineties, the conditions for its ascent had crystallized. The social promises of Congress had faded, markets and money filled the air-waves, customary expectations and inhibitions were eroded. In such conditions, anomic modernization unleashed a classic reaction of religious compensation.[52] The time for Hindutva, the vision of a revolutionary fighter incarcerated by the Raj on the Andamans before Gandhi ever set political foot in India, had come.

The rise of the BJP was greeted with intense alarm by most of the country's intellectuals, many of whom saw the party and its mentor the RSS as akin to an Indian version of fascism. This was a category mistake – there was no working-class threat, no economic slump, no revanchist drive, to produce any subcontinental equivalent of the inter-war scene in Europe.[53] It overlooked not only the distinct social matrix of Hindutva, but the ideological setting in which it could flourish. Indian secularism of the post-Independence period had never sharply separated state and religion, let alone developed any systematic critique of Hinduism. But by the eighties, it had come under fire from neo-nativist thinkers as an alienated elitism, insufficiently attuned to popular sensibilities and practices of devotion that Gandhi had intuitively understood, and

---

52 For a commanding analysis of this dynamic, see Achin Vanaik, *The Furies of Communalism: Religion, Modernity and Secularization*, London-New York, 1997, pp. 270–274.

53 Vanaik has also provided the most powerful critique of assimilations of the Sangh to fascism: *The Furies of Communalism*, pp. 255–270.

Subaltern Studies would later defend and illustrate. Still, the vocal anti-secularism of Ashis Nandy, T.N. Madan and others remained a minority trend within intellectual opinion, if one that enjoyed high visibility and real influence.

Much more widespread was – and is – another discourse, embellishing Hinduism as preeminently a faith of tolerant pluralism and peaceable harmony, its teeming multiplicity of different deities, beliefs and rituals a veritable template for a modern multi-culturalism. For Amartya Sen and others, indeed, no other religion has so capaciously included even atheism in its repertoire, along with monotheism, polytheism, pantheism and any other sort of theism. In this version, secularism cannot be at odds with a Hinduism whose values are so close to its own. Of course, just because Hinduism is so ecumenical a religion, intolerant or aggressive strains may perforce also find accommodation within its embrace. But with a sufficiently open mind, these can be transformed into their opposite. Sen tells us that 'no matter what the "message" of the *Bhagavad-Gita* is meant to be' (*sic*), Arjuna's arguments against killing are 'not really vanquished' by Krishna – inviting us to believe it irrelevant that Arjuna ends by agreeing with Krishna and kills as enjoined. Since Sen's grandfather 'identified an overarching liberality as part and parcel of the basic Hindu approach', why trouble ourselves with what what can only be less basic? 'It is not particularly worthwhile', Sen explains, 'to enter into a debate over whether the liberal, tolerant and receptive traditions within Hinduism may in any sense be taken to be more authentic than the narrower and more combative interpretations that have been forcefully championed by present-day Hindu politics'.[54]

---

54 *The Argumentative Indian*, pp. 5, 46, 49.

A secularism as spavined as this presents small obstacle to Hindutva. Long before Sen, its originator Savarkar cast the generous mantle of Hinduism over atheists, and his successors have had no difficulty turning the tropes of Indo-tolerant pluralism into maxims of their own. The BJP does not oppose, but upholds secularism, for 'India is secular because it is Hindu'.[55] Its theorists have little reason to fear a debate others decline. 'About twenty-five words in an inscription of Asoka', Nirad Chaudhuri once observed, 'have succeeded in almost wholly suppressing the thousands in the rest of the epigraphy and the whole of Sanskrit literature which bear testimony to the incorrigible militarism of the Hindus' – more accurately, their rulers and bards – among whom, between the stele of Ashoka and the conversion of Gandhi, 'there is not *one word* of non-violence in the theory and practice of statecraft'.[56] Generalization for generalization, who could doubt which Bengali judgement is the more historical?

Overt encapsulation of the nation by religion has come later in India than it did in Ireland or Israel, but the prior 'accommodations' – in the technical Jesuit sense – of Hinduism by a world of lay officials and intellectuals were one of its enabling conditions. 'Myths have a way of running away with their proponents' an Indian critic of this outlook, of whom there have not been that many, has remarked: 'Belief in the essentially secular character of the modern Indian state and society can often be little more than an exercise in self-congratulation which overlooks or rationalizes the sectarian religious outlook pervading large areas of contemporary social and political practice'. The result is a blurring of ideological boundaries to

---

55 Radhika Desai, 'Forward March of Hindutva Halted?', *New Left Review* 30, November–December 2004, p. 62.

56 *The Continent of Circe*, London 1965, p 98.

a point where the BJP appropriates 'the languge of secularism', Congress makes a 'studied espousal of so-called soft *Hindutva*', and the Communist parties 'proffer and publicize versions of a "purer" and "truer" Hinduism closer to popular religion as they understand it'.[57]

In such a process of competitive desecularization, as another analyst has termed it, the initial advantage could only lie with the BJP. Its breakthrough came in 1992 with a national campaign to demolish the mosque at Ayodhya desecrating the supposed birth-place of Rama, the only mass political mobilization, something of which Congress had long ceased to be capable, that India has seen for decades. Culminating in the triumphant destruction of the mosque, as the Congress government stood by, the dynamism of this operation gave the BJP the momentum that put it into office in Delhi by the end of the decade. But its arrival at the turn of the century as a ruling party was not a straightforward jump from the springboard of Ayodhya, nor a progress that left it structurally unaltered. Its strongholds had always lain in the Hindi-speaking belt of North India, a narrower regional base than that of Congress, and one incapable of delivering a parliamentary majority on its own. That was one obvious barrier to replacing Congress as India's dominant party. But there was another and more important obstacle it faced, from a different direction.

In the time of Nehru and for twenty years after him, Congress had ruled a segmented society, divided vertically and horizontally by caste, which rarely coincided across regions.[58]

---

57 G. Balachandran, 'Religion and Nationalism in Modern India', in Kaushik Basu and Sanjay Subrahmanyam, (eds) *Unravelling the Nation: Sectarian Conflict and India's Secular Identity*, New Delhi 1996, pp. 83, 126.

58 'The common impression that caste became a major factor in Indian politics only in the late 1960's is false', Radhika Desai has observed, in an

At the summit of this hierarchy, and at the controls of the state machine, were Brahmins. Beneath them, in that epoch, the least privileged castes comprising the majority of the population, pinioned in their hereditary stations, were the passive foundations of a huge democracy run by an elite without inconveniences from below. The Emergency imposed by Nehru's daughter not only released into being the BJP, it also cracked the carapace of the Congress system of caste subordination, wealthy farmers breaking away from it to lead the rebellion that brought the first non-Congress coalition to power in 1977. Fifteen years later, synchronized this time with the take-off of the BJP, caste erupted in full flow onto the political scene. The Constitution had mandated reservations in public employment by the central government for 'Scheduled Castes' and 'Scheduled Tribes' – *dalits* and *adivasis* – fixed initially at 12.5 and 5 per cent, later increased to 15 and 7.5 per cent. There matters stood, when the Janata coalition that briefly followed the Emergency produced a report from a commission headed by B.P. Mandal, a wealthy *shudra* from Bihar, recommending that other lower castes, amounting (it claimed) to over half the population, should be accorded 27 per cent of public sector jobs. On returning to power a year later, Congress would have none of this, and it was not until another Janata-style coalition

---

outstanding analysis of the mutations of caste hierarchy and ideological adaptations to them: 'The caste politics which emerged after 1967 did not mark the *first* assertion of the political power of these groups. It had long been effectively exercised from *within* the Congress party'. Simply, the penetration of capitalism into the countryside transformed 'the stuation wherein the dominant castes acted to preserve their hegemony locally through a maze of patronage structures that linked them to the subordinate castes', unleashing a new dynamic. 'The Cast(e) of Anti-Secularism', in Mushirul Hasan, *Will Secular India Survive?* Gurgaon 2004, pp. 197, 199–200.

was, again briefly, in office that the Mandal quota became law, over furious upper caste opposition in North India, in 1992.

The upshot was to galvanize an entire spectrum of hitherto apathetic, resigned or intimidated lower castes into active political life, transforming the landscape of Indian democracy. In short order, a coalition of two parties, one mobilizing *dalits* and the other OBCs, captured UP – much the largest state in the country – a year later, and within another two years, Lucknow had the first *dalit* Chief Minister in history, the redoubtable Mayawati, who has ruled the roost, alternating with her OBC rival, for the larger part of the time since. Congress has never recovered in what was once Nehru's electoral fief, his great-grandson crashing to humiliation there a few months ago. The upheaval in UP was the most spectacular expression of a new political scene, but elsewhere caste parties and factions sprouted across the land, disrupting traditional arrangements and drawing suppressed forces into play. What this development has wrought, unquestionably, is an impressive social deepening of Indian parliamentarism, whose roots now reach much further down into popular soil than before. For some, like the French scholar Christophe Jaffrelot, it represents a rise of the lower classes amounting to a 'silent revolution', if one yet to be fully consummated.[59]

But castes are not classes. Constructed by religion and divided by occupation, they are denizens of a universe of

---

59   Christophe Jaffrelot, *India's Silent Revolution: The Rise of the Lower Castes in North India*, New York 2003, pp. 494–496: 'the rise to power of the lower castes is not irreversible and linear'. Jaffrelot also points out that as these gain increasing footholds in political life and bureaucratic employment, the well-off and well-educated are recouping their power through the growing weight of the private economy, and the hollowing out of parliamentary decision by technocratic elites at the actual controls of state policy.

symbolism governed by customary rituals and taboos. State and market have loosened the frontiers between them, but when it came, political activism would all but inevitably acquire a distortingly symbolic twist. Job reservations are material benefits. The jobs, overwhelmingly in the lowest rungs of the bureaucracy, typically go to the highest layers within each caste, all of which are internally stratified. But since total public employment accounts for a mere 4 to 5 per cent of the labour force, they could be little more than a drop in the ocean of destitution and unemployment; if the more precious and bitterly fought over for that. Since regional reservations can be much higher than the national ceiling of 49.5 per cent set by the Supreme Court, elections at state level readily become 'job auctions' in which castes, often conglomerates of *jatis* cobbled together for the occasion, compete ferociously with each other for the spoils of office, in disregard of any logic of wider, let alone national solidarities. 'Castes have no permanent friends when it comes to politics':[60] electoral alliances of Brahmins and Kshatriyas with Untouchables against OBCs can be sealed in one part of the country, while higher-caste armies wage vicious rural war on dalits in another.

In driving this Hobbesian free-for-all, recognition – the quest for dignity – trumps redistribution, leaders gratifying followers with symbols of esteem rather than the substance of emancipation. Mayawati's erection of a 150,000 statues of

---

60 Dipankar Gupta, 'The Certitudes of Caste: When Identity Trumps Hierarchy', in Gupta (ed), *Caste in Question: Identity or Hierarchy?*, New Delhi 2004, p. xvi. In the apt formulation of Javeed Alam, as castes themselves become increasingly differentiated with capitalist development, 'fragments of these communities act within the public sphere as the equivalent of the egoistic induviduals in the competitive world of bourgeois possessiveness'. See his 'Handling Difference: the Right to a Way of a Life and Multi-Culturalism in India'.

Ambedkar, not to speak of two hundred effigies of the elephant symbol of her party and of herself (the largest 24-feet high, and like the rest covered in pink polythene as the state went to the polls in March, on orders from the Election Commission, so as not to beguile or distract voters), at the cost of more schools and heath-care, offers an extreme case of this identity politics, which does not seek to abolish caste, as Ambedkar had wanted, but to affirm it. Awakening as voters, the poor and not so poor activate hereditary enclosures as political communities rather dissolving them. Within these enclosures, internally far more hierarchical than equal, the identities are ascribed and conformity to them enforced. Historically, the political philosopher Javeed Alam has pointed out, caste was a form of collective unfreedom from which it was more difficult for individuals to escape than slavery or serfdom.[61] The traces of that remain.

Economic and educational development, however uneven, have weakened caste barriers. But crossing them is still taboo for the vast majority of the population, three quarters of whom reject intercaste marriage, as do well over half those with higher education.[62] Nor has the actual lot of *dalits*, exposed to violence and misery across India, changed in pace with either the formal ideology of citizenship or their electoral clout at the polls.[63]

---

61 'Classes Trapped in Castes: the Left's Ongoing Predicament in India', paper presented at Columbia University, April 2010.

62 Edward Luce, *In Spite of the Gods: The Strange Rise of Modern India*, London 2006, p. 143.

63 For a comprehensive review of the upshot of programmes of 'compensatory discrimination', see Oliver Mendelsohn and Marika Vicziany, *The Untouchables: Subordination, Poverty and the State in Modern India*, Cambridge 1998, pp. 118–146, who conclude that their effect 'does not begin to address the overall problem of Untouchable poverty or social disadvantage': p. 145. Already in the mid-eighties, Marc Galanter was noting that 'few direct benefits have reached the vast mass of landless labourers in the villages'; *Competing Equalities: Law and the Backward*

Castes continue to be, as they have always been, and Ambedkar saw, one of the purest negations of any notion of liberty and equality, let alone fraternity, imaginable. That the Indian state has never lifted a juridical finger to do away with them, but in seeking only to ameliorate, has if anything legally entrenched them, says more about its secularism than the omission of any reference to it in the Constitution, or the belated passage of an amendment professing it, by way of adorning the Emergency. But as they have become increasingly powerful lobbies, with the peculiar dynamism of hybrid voluntary-hereditary associations, castes are more than the ever the pediments of Indian democracy. No longer inert but vigilant, in yet more radically segmenting its vast electorate they are what most fundamentally stabilizes it.

The BJP, as a party aiming to unify the nation under its true Hindu banners, thus found, just as its momentum was increasing, caste blocking its path. At the time, its onslaught at Ayodhya was often read as a counter-blow to the arrival of Mandal, mobilizing the rage of upper caste youth against impending loss of privileges. There may have been some truth in this, but if so, a course correction soon followed. Realizing that it could not hope to win national power without attracting middle and lower castes, it set about broadening its appeal, and by the time of its first major electoral success in 1998, won 42 per cent of the OBC vote in North India. But regional parties, composed of heteroclite caste blocs, by now commanded too much of the landscape for it to have any chance of taking the place of Congress of old, itself now reduced to a remnant of its former self. In the last three national elections, the two parties combined have never won so much as half the total

---

Classes in India, New Delhi 1984, p. 551.

vote. Coalition with an array of regional parties has become a requirement of rule at the centre.

With it has come a large measure of convergence between Congress and the BJP in government, each pursuing at home a neo-liberal economic agenda, as far as their allies will allow them, and abroad a strategic rapprochement with the United States. Culturally, they now bathe in a common atmosphere in which religious insignia, symbols, idols, and anthems are taken for granted in commercial and official spaces alike. Organizationally, they are not so similar, since the BJP possesses real cadres and members, Congress little more than a memory of them. Ideologically, too, their appeals are distinct, as are their social bases. Congress may tack towards confessionalism, but it can still rely on Muslim and *adivasi* vote-banks by pointing to the BJP as a greater sectarian danger, and invoke a vague social paternalism to garner votes among the poor. The BJP may tack towards secularism, but it can rely on the fervour of the devout and the attraction of a more muscular nationalism to an upwardly mobile middle-class. Practically, the differences are less. Where communalism suits them, there is little to choose between the two. More died in the pogrom of 1984 in Delhi covered by Congress, than of 2002 in Gujarat covered by the BJP, although the the latter's active political complicity was greater. Neither compare with the massacres in Hyderabad under Nehru and Patel. Well-wishers abroad occasionally express hopes for a Grand Coalition uniting the two major parties in the service of modernizing reforms to bring the country up to scratch, as understood in Washington and Brussels, but the *raison d'etre* of each resists this.

With the morphing under pressure from below of the political system into one resembling the Irish or Israeli pattern,

has come plummeting levels of parliamentary personnel
and conduct. Pervasive corruption dates back to the third
generation of Nehru family rule, mired in a massive arms pro-
curement scandal, and the regime of Narasimha Rao, the first
to purchase a vote of confidence in the Lok Sabha with millions
in cash for defections to the government. Under the current
incumbent, Manmohan Singh, it has reached an all time high,
with the defalcation from the public purse of some $40 billion
in crooked telecom contracts alone, while the Prime Minister –
everywhere lauded as the image of probity – looked the other
way. As the costs of securing a seat in parliament have risen
vertically, so it has increasingly become a club of the super-rich:
one out of five MPs is a dollar millionaire, and the total assets
of its 543 members can be reckoned at $2 billion, in a society
where over half the population lives on less than $2 dollars a
day.[64] Indiscriminate criminality is the concomitant phenomenon. In the present Lok Sabha, some 150 MPs – over a quarter
of the house – have a total of more than 400 criminal charges
against them. At state level, the statistics are more extreme. In
2010, Bihar held elections that were widely hailed as a triumph
for the clean government of Nitish Kumar, a well-respected ally
of the BJP. Of the newly refreshed Legislative Assembly, nearly
half – 110 out of 243 members – had criminal charges against
them, including murder, kidnapping and extortion.[65]

With a political class of this calibre, it is no surprise that
the Lok Sabha should now debate the nation's affairs for just
a third of the time it used to spend on them. Nor that nepo-
tism should have reached a point where over a third of all
Congress MPs have inherited their seats by family connexion –

64 See National Election Watch, *Analysis of MPs of the 15th Lok Sabha*, New
Delhi 2009.
65 *The Economic Times*, 25 November 2010.

twice the figure for the BJP – and every single one of them under the age of thirty-five.[66] In India democracy had never extended from government far into the parties contending for it, which were always run from the top down. Today, however, many have become something other than the oligarchic organizations into which Ostrogorsky and Michels thought all political parties must sooner or later turn. With the exception of the Communists and the BJP, they have become family firms competing for market shares of the electorate and so access to public office. The first of the major regional dynasties, setting the pattern for so many others, dates from the capture of the DMK in Tamilnadu by the Karunanidhi patriarch at the turn of the seventies. But the *fons et origo* of the transmission of power by bloodline came, of course, at national level, with Nehru's complaisance at the installation of his daughter in pole position to take over after him. This was the authoritative example, set at the apex of the Union, that legitimized the feudalism of hereditary succession at the rungs lower down; nowhere more pitifully than in Kashmir, where once restored to office and obedience in the seventies, Abdullah – a leader ultimately as disastrous for his people as any Abbas – passed a franchise for compliant enrichment to his offspring, who handed it on to his offspring, now a crony of the Nehru great-grandson. Of the ensuing scenery, André Béteille, the doyen of Indian sociologists, has written that the 'abject surrender' of Congress to a single family, corrupting all other parties, has done irreparable harm to Indian democracy, poisoning the wells of public life.[67]

Among so many degenerative symptoms in the executive and legislatures alike, one antibody in the constitution has

---

66 See the calculations in Patrick French, *India: A Portrait*, London 2011, pp. 118–120.

67 *Chronicles of Our Time*, New Delhi 2000, p 333.

stood out. The Supreme Court, which had not played a particularly distinguished role under Nehru, disgraced itself by
rubber-stamping the Emergency. Thereafter, spurred by the
reaction against it and no doubt ashamed of its past servility,
the Court has moved in the opposite direction, becoming the
principal breakwater in India against threats to liberty, abuses
of power and theft of public goods. In two landmark changes,
the Court has made it more difficult for the centre to overturn
elected governments in the regions by imposing Presidential
Rule, and started to accept 'public interest litigation', allowing
ordinary citizens and associations in civil society to bring suits
before it against public authorities.

Today, the Court is so pro-active that it can not only
annul laws passed in the Indian Parliament if it decides they
are unconstitutional, the normal prerogative of a Supreme
Court, but demand that Parliament pass laws it determines
are urgently needed – a juridical innovation without precedent
in any other country. The current bench has harried Congress
and its Prime Minister on the telecoms scandal, and shows no
sign of being willing to sponge its implications away. The Court,
now self-recruiting, has become the most powerful judiciary
on earth. It has acquired such an abnormal degree of authority
because of the decay of the representative institutions around it.
Even admirers are aware of the risks. In the graphic phrase of
Upendra Baxi, India's leading legal scholar and one of the first to
bring a public interest suit before the court, it is 'chemotherapy
for a carcinogenic body politic'.[68] So long as the malady persists,
few Indians would think the country better off without it.

---

68 'Introduction' to S.P. Sathe, *Judicial Activism in India*, New Delhi 2002,
p. xvi. Baxi himself, a mordant intellect with small time for cant of any
kind, prefers 'social action legislation' to the conventional 'public interest legislation', which he terms a misnomer. Of the subject treated by the

The tidal wave of corruption in Indian public life has, of course, been in part a by-product of the neo-liberal turn of the state since the nineties, and the faster growth it has unleashed. The country now occupies a prominent place in every prospectus of BRIC powers, where the Indian economy is the second largest in size, though in many ways strange in shape. Manufacturing is not its pile-driver. Services account for over half of GDP, in a society where agriculture accounts for more than half the labour-force, yet less than a fifth of GDP. Over 90 per cent of total employment is in the informal sector, a mere 6 or 8 per cent in the formal sector, of which two-thirds are to be found in government jobs of one kind or another. In India cultivable land is 40 per cent more abundant than in China, but on average agricultural yields are 50 per cent lower. The population is younger and growing faster than in China, but the demographic dividend is not being cashed: for ten million new entrants into the labour force each year, just five million jobs are being created.[69] The greatest economic success of the past twenty years has been achieved in IT, where firms of global impact have emerged. But its employment effect is nugatory: perhaps two per of the labour force. Even in high-technology industries, average labour productivity appears to be little more than a third of Chinese levels.[70]

---

generally optimistic book he introduces, he comments: 'judicial activism in India presents stories both of complicity with dominant power formations and ways of insurrection', adding that when a colleague recast the mission of such activism in Gandhi's metaphor of 'wiping every tear from each Indian eye, I had publicly to remind him, with great affection, that a tattered judicial handkerchief may only result in aggravated trachoma': pp. xii, xviii – words of more than subcontinental application.

69 Edward Luce, *In Spite the Gods*, pp. 48, 342, 344.

70 Pranab Bardhan. *Awakening Giants, Feet of Clay: Assessing the Economic Rise of India and China*, Princeton 2010, p. 130.

Nonetheless, growth averaged some 7.7 per cent in the first decade of this century, with savings rising to 36 per cent of GDP – double the respective rates of Brazil. But if the comparator is China, with roughly the same size of population and similar starting-point in the fifties, India scarcely shines, as Pranab Bardhan has shown in his masterly analytic survey of the two countries, *Awakening Giants, Feet of Clay*. Per capita income in India is about quarter of that in China, and inequality is significantly higher even than in the notoriously polarized PRC. India may have fewer billionaires than China, but they are also richer, and their share of national wealth far greater: just 66 resident billionaires control assets worth more than a fifth of the country's GDP. Capital at large is three times more concentrated than in the United States. At the other end of the social scale, poverty has declined since the nineties, though not more rapidly than in the seventies and eighties, and if measured by the World Bank line of a miserable $1.25 a day, still stood at over two-fifths of the population in 2005. Infant mortality is three times as high as in China. Under-nourishment is much worse even than in sub-Saharan Africa, afflicting over half of all Indian children under the age of five. In eleven Indian states, four-fifths of the population are afflicted with anaemia. For the most party, the corrective role of the state is minimal. Two-thirds of all government subsidies – for food, fuel, electricity – go the relatively well-off, mainly rich farmers. Over 80 per cent of expenditure on health care is private. One out of every five children never goes to school. Military expenditure virtually equals spending on all anti-poverty programmes combined.[71]

---

71 Bardhan, *Awakening Giants* pp. 7, 12, 34, 91, 94, 97, 105, 109, 112, 134–135; for undernourishment and anaemia, see *Financial Times*, 23 December 2010; for billionaires, *International Herald Tribune*, 10 December 2010; for military spending, Luce, *In Spite of the Gods*, p. 82.

Yet the Indian state is still, for big business and foreign investors alike, a far from satisfactory steward of the country's interests. Neo-liberal the direction of every government since the nineties may have been, but the pace has often been halting and the road strewn with obstacles. The *dirigiste* instincts of an unregenerate bureaucracy and the populist demagogy of too many politicians have, in this view, hampered normal progress to freer markets. Banking remains largely controlled by the state. There has been little privatization, even of such important industries as coal. Barriers to trade persist, tariffs still twice as high as in China. Quotas limiting international stake-holders have not been abolished. Why be surprised, then, that FDI runs so low, that the two-million-strong Indian expatriates – the richest of all immigrant communities in the United States – fail to invest in the homeland as gladly as overseas Chinese have done, or that the Mumbai conglomerates put so much money into buying up auto or steel in Britain, where Tata is now the largest private employer in the UK?

What such frustrations express is the intractable brake that Indian democracy has so far placed on the fullest expansion of Indian capital. The poor outvote the rich, the villages the cities, the slums the suburbs.[72] At once activated and segregated by caste, the deprived have never been able to achieve any real redistribution of national income, their drive for recognition typically contenting itself with symbolic representation in the political firmament, with little reaction at its lack of practical consequence. Comparing India and China from another angle, one of the most lucid political minds of the subcontinent, Pratap Bhanu Mehta, has observed that in the People's Republic, where there is no democracy, Communist rule is based on

---

72   Yogendra Yadav, 'Representation', in Niraja Gopal Jayal and Pratap Bhanu Mehta, *Oxford Companion to Politics in India*, New Delhi 2010, p. 354.

output legitimacy – it is accepted by the masses for the material benefits it takes great care to deliver them, however unequally, whereas in India, democracy allows just the opposite: an input legitimacy from the holding of free elections, that thereby dispenses the political class from distributing much more than confetti to the masses who have elected them.[73]

Commentators now complain as regularly of legislative deadlock in Delhi as they do in Washington. But the underlying reasons are quite different. What the Indian impasse reflects is the political contradiction at the core of the system between, as Zoya Hasan has crisply put it, 'the frustration of the majority of citizens with governments they vote in but do not control, and the smug indifference of elites and middle classes towards governments they do not vote in, but control.'[74] Neoliberal precepts have the favour of the latter. Yet the former still continue, negatively, to inhibit too provocative a dismantling of the arrangements of an earlier, more paternalist system of rule. Worse, from the standpoint of the stock-market and the technocrats of a liberalization to empower it, even positive legislation cannot be wholly insulated from the pressure of a vast destitute electorate. In 2005, when Congress still depended on Communist votes for a majority in Parliament, a National Rural Employment Guarantee Act (NREGA) was passed, assuring any household in the countryside a hundred days labour a

---

73 'The State of Indian Democracy', in Rajesh Basrur (ed), *Challenges to Democracy in India*, New Delhi 2009, pp. 50–51.

74 'Indian Democracy and Social Inequalities', Basrur (ed), *Challenges to Democracy*, p. 143. For a formulation that can be taken as complementary, see Achin Vanaik's fireworks in 'The Paradoxes of Indian Politics', in Achin Vanaik and Rajeev Barghava, *Understanding Contemporary India: Critical Perspectives*, New Delhi 2010, p. 349: 'The countryside decides which political force comes to power. The cities and towns decide the direction the polity takes'.

year at the legal minimum wage on public works, with at least a third of these jobs for women. It is work for pay, rather than a direct cash transfer scheme as in Brazil, to minimize the danger of money going to those who are not actually the poor, and so ensure it reaches only those willing to do the work. Denounced by all right-thinking opinion as debilitating charity behind a façade of make-work, it was greeted by the middle-class like 'a wet dog at a glamorous party', in the words of one of its architects, the Belgian-Indian economist Jean Drèze. Unlike the *Bolsa Família* in Brazil, the application of NREGA was left to state governments rather than the centre, so its impact has been very uneven and incomplete, wages often paid lower than the legal minimum, for days many fewer than a hundred. [75] Works performed are not always durable, and as with all other social programmes in India, funds are liable to local malversation.

But in scale NREGA now represents the largest entitlement programme in the world, reaching some 40 million rural households, a quarter of the total in the country. Over half of these *dalit* or *adivasi*, and 48 per cent of its beneficiaries are women – double their share of casual labour in the private sector. Such is the demand for employment by NREGA in the countryside that it far outruns supply. A National Survey Sample for 2009–2010 has revealed that 45 per cent of all rural households wanted the work it offers, of whom only 56 per cent got it.[76] What NREGA has started to do, in the formulation Drèze has taken from

---

75 Reetika Khera (ed), *The Battle for Employment Guarantee*, New Delhi 2011. In 2006–2007, 'NREGA generated only 17 days of employment per rural household on average' – in many states less than 10 days, and in all districts sampled, 'the provisions and guidelines were routinely violated': pp. 19, 64.

76 Puja Dutta, Rinku Murgai, Martin Ravallion, Dominique Van der Walle, 'Does India's Employment Guarantee Scheme Guarantee Employment?', *Economic and Political Weekly*, 21 April 2012, pp. 57, 62.

Ambedkar, is break the dictatorship of the private employer in the countryside, helping by its example to raise wages even of non-recipients. Since inception, its annual cost has risen from $2.5 to over $8 billion, a token of its popularity. This remains less than 1 per cent of GDP, and the great majority of rural labourers in the private sector are still not paid the minimum wage due them.

Conceived outside the party system, and accepted by Congress only when it had little expectation of winning the elections of 2004, the Act eventually had such popular demand behind it that the Lok Sabha adopted it nem con. Three years later, with typical dishonesty, the Manmohan regime renamed it as 'Gandhian' to fool the masses that Congress inspired it.[77] The contrast in origin and scope with the *Bolsa Família* underlines the major difference between the two great tropical democracies. NREGA is being applied in structurally far less favourable conditions. Brazil had a Workers' Party born from a militant labour struggles, and a leader of these, committed to and capable of coherent social reform. In India, the Communist tradition is long splintered in three directions, and trade-unions muster no more than a tiny 3 per cent of the labour force. Caste, not class, and alas, least of all the working-class, is what counts most in popular life, at once sustaining Indian democracy and draining it of reconstructive energy.

If the poor remain divided against themselves, and workers are scattered and ill-organized, what of other sources of opposition within the political system? The new middle-class has turned against mega-corruption, but is scarcely foreign to the

---

77   In reality, BJP governments have to date had a notably better record than Congress governments in implementing NREGA – 'on the whole the BJP seems to have welcomed Congress's orphan with open arms': *The Battle for Employment Guarantee*, p. 35.

bribe and the wink, let alone favours to kin, at its own level of advantage. Besotted with a culture of celebrity and consumption, on spectacularly vapid display in much of the media, and to all appearances hardening in collective egoism, it is no leaven in the social order. The intelligentsia is another matter. There, India possesses a range and quality of minds that perhaps no other developing society in world, and not that many developed ones, can match. Whether working inside or outside the Union, they form an interconnected community of impressive acuity and distinction. In what kind of relationship do they stand to their country? Intellectuals are often held, quite wrongly, to be critical by definition. But in some societies, the mistake has become internalized as a self-conception or expectation, and so it probably is for most Indian intellectuals. How far do they live up to it?

Generalizations here are bound to be fallible. But an approximate assessment is perhaps possible all the same. What is clear is that attitudes differ according to issues, along a gradient that has a logic of its own. So far as Indian society at large is concerned, it is safe to say an overwhelming consensus is highly critical. It would be difficult to identify the social disorder or iniquity that has not been subjected to unsparing scrutiny. Hunger, misery, illiteracy; inequality of every kind, sexual discrimination, economic exploitation; corruption, commercialization, fanaticism; the spreading of the slums, the looting of the environment – a detailed scholarship of anger or disgust covers virtually all. The passionate indictments of a great deal of this landscape in recent essays by Ramachandra Guha, the eminent critical liberal who is India's leading contemporary historian – they extend also to his country's pretensions to great power status – are eloquent of a widely shared sensibility.[78]

78 See, *inter alia*, 'Will India Become a Superpower?', *Outlook*, 30 June 2008;

Society is one thing; politics, although never disconnected from it, another. What of the claims of the 'idea of India', or what can equally well be called the Indian Ideology – the triune values of democracy, secularity and unity? Here the ether alters noticeably. But the response to the three is not the same: with each, the critical quotient is distinct. Indian democracy, although so often ritually loaded like a local idol with garlands as if it were a miracle, is on the whole treated with far less superstition than the rites might suggest. Indeed, few countries enjoy such a copious and sophisticated body of political science, bearing on so many aspects of its electoral and constitutional life. The six hundred folio pages of the recent *Oxford Companion to Politics in India*, edited by Niraja Gopal Jayal and Pratap Bhanu Mehta, are impressive testimony enough to that. Empirical and theoretical approaches combine, in a spirit that is typically both analytical and critical. From Mehta's own sharp *Burden of Democracy* to Guha's judgement at the end of his *India After Gandhi* that the country is at best a '50 per cent democracy', few intellectuals have lost sight of flaws and limitations in the Indian version of representative government.

Yet compared with social criticism, political critique is typically less comprehensive, and less searching. For no political system, however democratic, consists just of its institutions of representation. They are always flanked and buttressed by its apparatuses of repression. Symptomatically, these are a conspicuous absence in the *Oxford Companion*, as elsewhere, where civil rights scarcely figure. Neither the long-standing barrage of liberticide laws in India – starting with the Preventive Detention Act rammed through by Nehru and Patel

'A Nation Consumed by the State', *Outlook*, 31 January 2011; 'India is Too Corrupt to Become a Superpower', *Financial Times,* 20 July 2001.

as early as February 1950, less than a month after the promulgation of the new Constitution, and stretching through the Armed Forces Special Powers Act (1958), Unlawful Activities Prevention Act (1967), Prevention of Insults to National Honour Act (*sic* 1971), Maintenance of Internal Security Act (1971), National Security Act (1980), Terrorism and Disruptive Activities Act (1985), Prevention of Terrorist Activities Act (2002), Unlawful Activities Amendment Act (2004) – nor the role and character of the Army, the Central Reserve Police Force, Border Security Force, Central Industrial Security Force, Home Guards, let alone the clandestine powers and activities of the Intelligence Bureau – a vast military, paramilitary and surveillance complex, totalling upwards of two million operatives – receive even passing mention in most of the literature on the world's largest democracy.

There are honourable exceptions. 'A staggering number of laws that sanction the use of coercive powers have been enacted in India' writes Arvind Verma. Noting that some 53,000 people were arrested under the Terrorism and Disruptive Activities Act, of whom just 434 could be convicted seven years later, he underlines some daily realities of Indian democracy: 'torture is routinely practised in most police stations and death in police custody is a frequent phenomenon', while – nominally outside the jails themselves – 'the police practice of getting rid of suspects through staged encounters is unfortunately all too common. Suspects against whom the police are unable to bring substantial evidence or those who are perceived to be dangerous are simply murdered'.[79] Nor, while the police are at work, have

79 Arvind Verma, 'Police Agencies and Coercive Power', in Ganguly et al. (eds), *The State of India's Democracy*, pp. 130–131, 135. Another forthright critic of this scene has been Paul Brass: see 'The Strong State and the Fear of Disorder', in Frankel (ed), *Transforming India*, pp. 60–88. Both scholars are based abroad.

the military been idle. In the sixties, the Army was deployed 'in aid of the civil power' some 476 times – in 1979–1980 alone, another 64 times; often 'openly stationed so as to provide a per-petual reminder, and on occasion an actual expression, of the fact that the existing social and political order in India is only to be challenged by its critics at their peril'.[80]

These are not matters on which the literature of miracu-lism cares to dwell. It is not only, however, in breadth of scope that even more level-headed accounts of the political system so often fall short, but depth of penetration too. There is no lack of ledgers registering assorted strengths and weaknesses of representative democracy in India, and arriving at different estimates of the balance between them. But Ambedkar's inau-gural error has yet to be corrected. Virtually all conventional analysis posits, as he did, a contradiction between society and polity, and explains imperfections in the latter, that he did not foresee, as effects of distortions in the former, of which he was bitterly aware. But the relationship between the two has always been more paradoxical than this. A rigid social hierarchy was the basis of original democratic stability, and its mutation into a compartmentalized identity politics has simultaneously deep-ened parliamentary democracy and debauched it. Throughout, caste is the cage that has held Indian democracy together, and it has yet to escape.

At secularity, taboos become stronger and the front of criticism narrows. In part, the reason lies in the political, and to some extent intellectual, chequerboard, of recent decades, where to question official secularism as a doctrine, for a wide mainstream, risks opening the gates not only to nativist snipers

---

80 Low, *Eclipse of Empire*, p. 152. See also Stephen Cohen, *The Indian Army*, New Delhi 1990, p 202.

but the troops of Hindutva. Yet the reflex of Belloc's 'Children, always cling to nurse, for fear of finding something worse', though real enough, is not the principal reason for a reluctance to tackle the sophisms and evasions of Indian secularism that makes the courage of its few true critics, preeminently the independent Marxist scholar Achin Vanaik, stand out all the more starkly. The larger explanation lies elsewhere, in the tensions of the relationship of so many Indian intellectuals to the traditional faith surrounding them. Even for non-believers in the ranks of Congress, once religion had fused with nation in the independence struggle, to demystify one was to damage the other. In the twenties the great Tamil iconoclast E.V. Ramasamy could declare: 'He who invented God is a fool. He who propagates God is a scoundrel. He who worships God is a barbarian'. He is still admired in his homeland. But an enemy of caste and of sexual inequality as fearless as this had no place in the construction of the Indian Union, which he resisted, and once it was consolidated, a stance like his became unthinkable for any politician with national ambitions. Intellectuals were under less constraint, but few cared to be too outspoken. On the whole, only *dalit* writers have broken ranks. For how could the stature of Gandhi as father of the nation not suffer if Hinduism was to be handled so brusquely?

To this political inhibition was added a cultural difficulty. Sociologically, Hinduism was not a realm of belief or practice separate from the rest of existence, but permeated it as the ubiquitous texture of popular life. How could even secular progressives affront it, without loss of human sympathy with the vast majority of their fellow citizens, and the symbols and ceremonies lending colour and meaning to their lives? Not only that. Like every other major religion, Hinduism also gave rise to a major reservoir of high culture – metaphysics, poetry and mathematics, in particular. To dismiss or under-value such riches of the subcontinental past could only be as a philistine a self-mutilation as would be a breezy ignorance of Christian art or thought in the West or the classical corpus in China. Preeminent among them, too, were the great epics of Hindu legend, the *Mahabharata* and the *Ramayana*, which unlike the *Odyssey* or the *Aeneid*, are still in such absolute command of popular imagination that their dramatization on television could not only mesmerize hundreds of millions of viewers, but occasion many a literal act of worship before the small screen. If Gandhi could in all seriousness advise Congress in 1947 that Partition was no more definitive than Ravana's abduction of Sita to Ceylon, where Rama would reclaim her; or the law minister of a Communist-supported government in Delhi, assuring the Supreme Court of his faith in the divinity of Rama, defer as potential sacrilege the dredging the Pamban channel across which Hanuman's monkey army built a bridge to rescue Sita – who should be impious enough to gainsay them? Accommodation of fervours like these, inspired by so popular a literary masterpiece, might be held common prudence on the part of a state equi- or flexi- distant from all religions. Indian secularism can encompass them all. Few are inclined to ask how many clothes it ever possessed, or what has become of them.

At the last of the Trimurti values, dissent comes close to vanishing altogether. Democracy may be imperfect, secularity ambiguous, but unity – of the nation and the land belonging to it – has become virtually untouchable. Here the heritage of the past has had its own weight. Hindu culture, exceptionally rich in epics and metaphysics, was exceptionally poor in history, a branch of knowledge radically devalued by the doctrines of *karma*, for which any given temporal existence on earth was no more than a fleeting episode in the moral cycle of the soul. No chronicles of more than local significance appear till the twelfth century,[81] over a millenium later than Herodotus or Sima Qian, and no *histoire raisonnée* as a cumulative body of writing ever emerged. Gandhi's dictum dismissing the worth of any memory of the past – 'history is an interruption of nature' – is a famous modern expression of this outlook. In such a his-toriographic vacuum, when the nationalist movement arose, legend encountered no barrier. 'In an overwhelmingly religious society', one subcontinental scholar has written, 'even the most clear-sighted leaders have found it impossible to distinguish romanticism from history and the latter from mythology', with the result that 'if the idea of India is suffused with religious and mythical meanings, so is the territory it covers' – Nehru explaining to Zhou Enlai that the *Mahabharata* entitled him to the Macmahon Line. Today the cult of Indian unity has typi-cally worked itself free from such mystical origins, territory as such becoming the bond unifying the nation, regardless of any religious – let alone ethnic or cultural – trappings. Meghnad Desai's *Rediscovery of India* is a recent example. In many ways a unusually free-spirited work, it dismantles not a few nation-alist myths, only to end with the purest hypostasization of another, in which the 'one element central to the narrative of

---

81 For a careful discussion of what historical materials have survived, see Michael Witzel, 'On Indian Historical Writing. The role of the Vaṃçâvaliś', *Journal of the Japanese Association for South Asian Studies*, No 2, 1990, pp. 1–57, a critique of blanket dismissals of any record of the past in the Sanskrit corpus, that nevertheless concludes: 'Historiography as a sepa-rate, impartial science, however, largely remains a lacuna in traditional Indian civilization'. In his recent *India: Brief History of a Civilization*, New York-London 2011, no less an authority than Thomas Trautmann has judged its contribution in this field too slight too warrant consideration.

nationhood' becomes simply 'territorial integrity', under whose idyllic shelter 'all Indians, as individuals, are willing to coexist under the same legal and constitutional system', 'all regions have agreed to be part of the Union', and 'all take part in the vibrant democratic process'.[82]

The reality is otherwise. There should be little need for any reminder of the fate of Kashmir, under the longest military occupation in the world. At its height, in the sixty years since it was taken by India, some 400,000 troops have been deployed to hold down a Valley population of five million – a far higher ratio of repression than in Palestine or Tibet. Demonstrations, strikes, riots, guerrillas, risings urban and rural, have all been beaten down with armed force. In this 'valley of scorpions', declared Jagmohan – proconsul for Nehru's daughter in Kashmir – 'the bullet is the only solution'.[83] The death toll, at a low reckoning, would be equivalent to the killing of four million people, were it India – more than double that, if higher estimates were accurate. Held fast by Nehru to prove that India was a secular state, Kashmir has demonstrated the exact opposite: a confessional expansionism. Today, the security complex that rules it under military command contains scarcely a Muslim, and jobs in the bureaucracy can be openly advertised for Hindus only. In what was supposed to be the show-case of India's tolerant multi-culturalism, ethnic cleansing has reduced Muslims, once a majority, to a third of the population of Jammu, and Hindu Pandits to a mere handful in the Valley.

---

82   *The Rediscovery of India*, pp. 451, 463.

83   Schofield, *Kashmir in the Crossfire*, pp. 244, 248. 'Every Muslim in Kashmir is a militant today', he raged, 'All of them are for secession from India'. A crony of Nehru's grandson Sanjay, Jagmohan's previous assignment was bulldozing the poor from their slums in Delhi during the Emergency.

How is this landscape received by the Indian intelligentsia? In late 2010, readers of the Indian press could find a headline 'Nobel Laureate takes India to task for tolerating tyranny'. Where would that be? Below, Amartya Sen uttered a plangent cry. 'As a loyal Indian citizen', he exclaimed, 'it breaks my heart to see the prime minister of my democratic country – and one of the most humane and sympathetic political leaders in the world – engaged in welcoming the butchers of Myanmar and photographed in a state of cordial proximity'.[84] Moral indignation is too precious an export to be wasted at home. That the democracy of his country and the humanity of his leader preside over an indurated tyranny, replete with torture and murder, within what they claim as their national borders, need not ruffle a loyal Indian citizen. If we turn to *The Argumentative Indian*, we find – in a footnote: 'the Kashmir issue certainly demands political attention on its own (I am not taking up that thorny question here)'.[85] Nor, we might infer from that delicate parenthesis, anywhere else either. Nobel prizes are rarely badges of political courage – some of infamy – so there is little reason for surprise at a silence that, in one form or another, is so common among Indian intellectuals.

Brazen celebration of India's good will in Kashmir, its peace troubled only by terrorists infiltrated from Pakistan, is a staple of the media more than the academy. There, discreet allusion to 'human rights abuses' that have marred the centre's performance are quite acceptable, excesses that any decent person must deplore. But any talk of self-determination is another matter, garlic to the vampire. Here more than just ordinary intellectual conformism is at work. To break ranks

---

84 'We Hear You, Michael Aris, Loud and Clear', *Outlook*, 15 November 2010, pp. 52–55.

85 *The Argumentative Indian*, p. 311.

on India's claim to Kashmir is to risk not only popular hysteria but legal repression, as Arundhati Roy – brave enough to speak of freedom for Kashmir – bears witness: to question the territorial integrity of the Union is a crime punishable at law. The same degree of pressure does not obtain outside the country, but Indian intellectuals abroad have not made notably better use of their greater freedom of expression. There the leading production comes from Sumantra Bose. *Kashmir: Roots of Conflict, Paths of Peace* (2003) does not embellish the record of Indian rule, and covers in some detail the insurgencies which broke out against it in the nineties, the extent of the assistance they received from Pakistan, and the way they were put down.

Descriptively, there is little it avoids. Prescriptively, however, it simply underwrites the status quo, on the grounds that the confessional and ethnic pattern in the region is now too complicated for self-determination to be applicable, and anyway India is not going to permit any such thing, so why not settle for the existing line of control, naturally assorted with appropriate placebos and human rights? Thus, on the one hand, 'The myth of freely and voluntarily given consent to Indian sovereignty is exploded by the appalling record of New Delhi-instigated subversion of democratic procedures and institutions and abuse of democratic rights in IJK over fifty years'. But on the other hand – immediately following, on the same page – 'That India's dismissal of the plebiscite [promised the UN in 1947] is fundamentally opportunistic does not detract from the reality that after more than fifty years of conflict [notice the way the description of the fifty years has changed in the space of two sentences], the plebiscite *is* indeed an obsolete idea'. Why so? 'Self-determination is untenable given realpolitik, the entrenched interests of states, and the internal social and political diversity of IJK and of J&K as a whole'. Even an independent Kashmir, let alone one that opted for Pakistan, 'would be seen as an intolerable loss of territorial integrity and sovereignty by Indian state elites and the vast majority of the Indian public'. Upshot? 'Erasing or redrawing the Line of Control in Kashmir is neither feasible nor desirable'. We hold what we have: 'The de facto Indian and Pakistani sovereignties over their respective areas of Kashmir cannot, should not and need not be changed'.

No Indian General could put it better. Bose, who worked as an understrapper for Strobe Talbott – second-in-command at the State Department and 'intimately involved in diplomacy on the South Asian subcontinent', in the era when Clinton was congratulating Russia on the 'liberation' of Grozny – situates his solution for Kashmir in a constructive wider vision, in which 'India's maturity and confidence as the world's largest and most diverse democracy' and 'well-founded aspiration to be an economic and political player of global stature' should be able to find the right partner across the border in a future 'relatively moderate Pakistan which happens to be strongly influenced by its relationship with the United States' (sic).[86] Translated: if only there were a Sadat or Mubarak in Islamabad, Kashmir could enjoy the blessings of another Oslo, and Delhi the good conscience of Tel Aviv.

---

86 *Kashmir: Roots of Conflict, Paths to Peace*, Cambridge Mass. 2003, pp. 167, 182, 207, 261, 265. From the same stable, this time directly introduced by Strobe Talbott as President of the Brookings Institution ('South Asia is of growing importance to Brookings as we seek to become a truly global think tank') comes Navnita Chadha Behera, *Demystifying Kashmir*, Washington 2006, who offers the ineffable reassurance: 'Though New Delhi has now and then strayed from its democratic, federal and secular commitments to the people in Jammu and Kashmir, over the years the Indian polity has developed a democratic resilience to learn from its mistakes': p. 30.

Looking North-East, attitudes are much the same, if typically rationales for them are adjusted to local conditions. There, the standard justification for military repression is that the various insurgent communities have always been far too small and isolated to be able to form independent states, and can only benefit from inclusion in the much more advanced Indian Union. The argument, like so much else in the national apologetics, is risible. Bhutan, in the same zone, is even more landlocked, and has a smaller population than either Nagaland, Manipur, Mizoram or even Meghalaya. Yet it is a perfectly viable independent state, with a seat at the United Nations like any other, and short of going the way of Sikkim, annexed by India in 1975, will continue to be so. What is true is that no break away from the Union is conceivable in this area, not because of any economic impossibility, but because Delhi can unleash overwhelming military force, as it has done for a half a century, to crush any attempt at secession, and can count on exhaustion eventually wearing out all resistance, as it cannot in Kashmir, where the alternatives of independence or inclusion in Pakistan have not left the Valley, and any free vote would prefer either to the Indian yoke.

The toll of the two occupations forms no part of the triune liturgy. But the cold truth is that the British massacre at Amritsar which ignited the first great mass movement of the independence struggle was a bagatelle compared with the accumulated slaughter by the Indian Army and paramilitary forces of their fellow-citizens, or those deemed such, since independence. The same could, of course, be said of many states that were once colonies, not least the US itself, where the price in human life of territorial integrity was far higher. Still, at the altar of Trimurti, costs are discounted inversely to gains.

Unity, whose moral and political deadweight is heavier, is safer from reproach than democracy or secularity.

An ideology, to be effective, must always in some measure answer to reality. The 'Idea of India' is not a mere tissue of myths. The coexistence of so many languages, the durability of parliamentary forms of government, the liveliness of cultural life, the vigour of much intellectual exchange, and elegance of social manners at their best, are all rightly matters of pride, out of which it has been fashioned. But the realities of the Union as a whole are more complex, many of them much darker. The Idea is a late mutant of Indian nationalism. Once any independent state has emerged from an anti-colonial struggle, however, what was once a discourse of awakening can easily become one of intoxication. In India that danger is great, both because of the size of the nation, and the particular character and outcome of the way it came into being. Across its borders lie the accusing facts of the states that did not become part of India, whose existence cannot be squared with much of the story it continues to tell itself, and still could bring that to a fatal end. Consoling themselves for domestic shortcomings, Indian intellectuals will often contrast the happier condition of their country with that of Pakistan. But given their respective starting-points, not to speak of the responsibility of the stronger in doing its best to sabotage the weaker from the outset, the comparison risks pharisaism. In any case, it is not always to Indian advantage. Though the military loom larger, today the media are more outspoken in Pakistan; though it is yet poorer, there is less undernourishment and better health care in Bangladesh. A more generous, more curious and more self-critical sense of their neighbours would become Indian attitudes better.

Needed above all is detachment from the totems of a romanticized past, and its relics in the present. The dynasty that still rules the country, its name as fake as the knock-off of a prestige brand, is the negation of any self-respecting republic. The party over which it presides has lost any *raison d'être* beyond clinging to its blood-line – now desperately pinning its hopes, after the flop of Nehru's weakling great-grandson, on his hard-bitten sister, if only she would hurry up and divorce her too obviously shady tycoon-husband. Congress had its place in the national liberation struggle. Gandhi, who had made it the mass force it became, called at independence for its dissolution. He was right. Since then the party has been a steadily increasing calamity for the country. Its exit from the scene would be the best single gift Indian democracy could give itself. The BJP is, of course, now a more dangerous force. But it is a real party, with cadres, programme, and a social base. It cannot be wished out of existence, because it represents a substantial political phenomenon which has to be fought as such, not the decaying fossil of one. So long as Congress lingers on paralytically, that will not occur. If it offers ultimate protection against Hindutva, why do more than just go on voting for it ? Why think of any radical reconstruction of the state over which it has so long presided?

The political ills that all well-meaning patriots now deplore are not sudden or recent maladies of a once healthy system. They descend from its original composition, through the ruling family and its affiliates, and the venerations and half-truths surrounding these and the organization enclosing them. Today, the largest statue in the world is being erected in Gujarat. The government commissioning it is BJP. But the giant it honours is a Congress leader, who wanted the RSS to join his party.

Vallabhbhai Patel will tower six hundred feet high, twice the height of the Statue of Liberty. Appropriately, his will be the Statue of Unity. Long preceding it are monumentalizations, no less immane, in words not stone, of his companions. It is time to put away these effigies, and all they represent.

Index of Names

Abbas, Mahmoud 160
Abdulhamid II 24
Abdullah, Sheikh Mohammed
  78–80, 85–87, 115–119,
  132, 160
Acton, Lord 89
Adivasis 137, 141
Aeneid 173
Afghanistan 10, 13
Agha Khan 25
Ahmad, Aijaz 74
Akbar (Mughal Emperor) 23, 82, 97
Aksai Chin plateau 124–129
Alam, Javeed 128, 155, 156
Alastair Lamb 80, 83, 116, 125
Algiers 119
Ambedkar, Bhimrao Ramji 5,
  37–38, 40–42, 52–53, 55–
  56, 89–90, 103, 112, 131,
  138–139, 143, 156–157,
  167, 171
Amritsar (Jallianwala Bagh mas-
  sacre) 26, 179
Anandamath 99
Andamans 149
Andhra Pradesh 145
Angola 115
Appalachia 120
Arjuna 150
Armed Forces Special Powers Act
  (AFSPA) 124, 135, 144, 170

Armenians 25
Arthasastra 108
Ashoka 151
Asquith, Anthony 13
Assam 71, 79, 120–123, 135
Assam Rifles 123
Attlee, Clement Richard 14, 62–63,
  65, 76, 84
Auchinleck, Claude (Field-Marshal)
  84, 89
Australia 45, 113
Ayodhya 22, 139, 152, 157
Azad, Maulana Abul Kalam 90

Badshah Khan 72–73, 85, 115–116
Bakshi, Ghulam Mohammed
  118–119
Baldwin, Stanley 46, 107
Baluchistan 57
Bangladesh 70, 115, 180
Baptists 121
Bardhan, Pranab 162–163
Bardoli 27, 29, 32–33, 35
Baxi, Upendra 161
Beijing 126
Belloc, Hilaire 172
Ben Bella, Ahmed 44
Bengal 4–5, 12, 16, 35, 58, 66,
  69–71, 73–74, 98–99, 108,
  117, 138, 141, 148
Ben Gurion, David 147

Bentham, Jeremy 51
Béteille, André 37, 160
Bhagavad-Gita 150
Bhave, Vinoba 45
Bhopal, Nawab of 83
Bhutan 121, 179
Bihar 16, 28, 50, 133, 153, 159
Birla, Ghanshyam Das 43, 71
BJP (Bharatiya Janata Party) 70,
        137, 147–149, 151–153,
        157–160, 167, 181
Blavatsky, Helena Petrovna (Mad-
        ame) 19
Boer War 28, 45
Bombay 16, 27, 41, 80, 108, 113,
        138
Border Security Force 170
Bose, Sarat Chandra 70
Bose, Subhas Chandra 43, 48, 52,
        57, 70, 131, 177–178
Bose, Sumantra 177
Brahmins 153, 155
Brazil 1, 110, 163, 166–167
BRIC 162
Brussels 158
Bulgaria 116
Burma 14, 48, 91, 115, 120–121,
        126

Cabinet Plan 95
Calais 134
Calcutta 27, 36, 43, 48, 62, 71–72,
        82, 108, 129
Caliphate 25–26, 35
Cambridge 52
Canada 45, 89, 107–108, 113
Caporetto 129
Carson, Edward 89
Cartland, Barbara 53
Central Asia 81
Central Industrial Security Force
        170
Central Reserve Police Force 170
Ceylon. See Sri Lanka

Chattopadhyay, Bankim Chandra
        99
Chaudhuri, Nirad 99, 151
Chauri Chaura 27, 33–34
Chiang Kai-shek 129
China 1, 10, 121, 124–129,
        162–164, 173
Churchill, Winston 46–47
CIA 126, 132, 143
Civil Disobedience 36–37, 43, 50,
        136
Clinton, William Jefferson 178
Colombo 47, 64
Columbia 52
Communism, Indian 4–5
Congo 115
Congress. See Indian National
        Congress
Constituent Assembly 62, 103,
        106–107, 112, 116, 138
Constitution 103–104, 106–109,
        111–114, 117, 128, 137–
        140, 142, 153, 157, 170
CPM (Communist Party-Marxist)
        4, 18, 141
Cripps, Stafford 14, 95
Curzon, Lord 16, 70, 101
Cyprus 76

Dail 148
Dalai Lama 126
Dalits 137, 141, 143
Deccan 10, 79
Dehra Dun 61, 126
Delhi iv, 7, 9, 11–12, 16, 36–37, 45,
        58, 61, 64, 73–76, 82–85,
        88, 90, 93, 97, 99, 103,
        107–108, 113, 116–118,
        120–126, 128–130, 132,
        134, 136, 139, 140–141,
        143–144, 149, 152, 155,
        157–161, 164–166, 171,
        173, 175, 177–179
Denning, Lord 75

Desai, Meghnad 8–9, 95, 174
De Valera, Eamon 107, 147
Discovery of India, The 7, 10, 52–53, 130
DMK 160
Dogra 78–79, 81, 116–118
Dogra forces 117
Drèze, Jean 166–167
Durga 99
Dyer, Reginald 26

Economic and Political Weekly 18, 166
Eden Commission 12
Emergency. See Emergency (1975–1977)
Emergency (1975–1977) 135–137, 148, 153, 157, 161, 175
Ethiopia 115

FBI 143
Fianna Fail 108, 147
Fine Gael 146
Flanders 28

Gandhi, Indira 8, 85, 136, 149
Gandhi, Mohandas (Mahatma) 2, 8–10, 16- 23, 25–46, 48–55, 57, 65, 71–73, 85–86, 89, 93–94, 97–98, 100–101, 106, 112, 121, 131, 135–136, 138, 147–149, 151, 169, 172–174, 181
Gandhi, Rajiv 149
Gandhi, Rajmohan 18
Gandhi, Sanjay 97, 152, 175
Ganges 147
Genghis Khan 133
George V 16
Germany 44, 48, 57
Gibbon, Edward 51
Goa 128
Gopal, Sarvepalli 89, 124, 130–132, 164, 169

Government of India Act (1935) 45, 107, 109
Grand Mufti 18
Greeks 54
Grozny 178
Guha, Ramachandra 8–9, 106, 168, 169
Gujarat 16, 23, 27, 33, 113, 158, 181
Gupta (dynasty) 10, 120
Gurdaspur 82–83
Gurkha 91, 123
Gurkhas 12–13, 143

Halifax, Lord 36, 45
Hanuman 173
Hardwar 23
Hari Singh (Maharajah of Kashmir) 78–79, 82–85, 87, 115–117, 121
Hasan, Mushirul 36, 74, 153
Hasan, Zoya 107, 165
Herodotus 174
Hindi 114, 152
Hind Swaraj 10, 20–23, 28, 31, 51, 101
Hindu Code Bill 138
Hinduism 23, 32, 37, 38, 40, 54, 90, 98, 112, 120, 139, 143–144, 149–152, 172
Hindu Mahasabha 70, 148
Hindutva 3, 89, 137, 149, 151–152, 172, 181
Hitler, Adolph 43
Home Guards 170
Hutton, Lord 75
Hyderabad 78–79, 82, 85, 87, 90–91, 158

IJK 177–178
Indian Army 12–13, 44, 83, 85–86, 90, 116, 143, 171, 179
Indian Civil Service 52
Indian National Army 48, 105
Indian National Congress 2, 10,

15–17, 22, 27, 32–36, 41–
49, 51–52, 55–68, 70–73,
76–79, 81, 83–84, 86, 88,–
91, 93–101, 105–108, 110,
112–118, 121–122, 131,
133–140, 142, 146–149,
152–154, 157–161, 165,
167, 172–173, 181
Indonesia 91, 92, 115
Intelligence Bureau 118, 124, 132,
134, 143, 170
IRA 148
Ireland 4, 21, 34–35, 46, 76, 89,
107–108, 146–147, 151
Irgun 148
Islam 23–24, 54, 80, 98, 137

Jabotinsky, Ze'ev 147
Jaffrelot, Christophe 154
Jamaica 104
Jammu 178
Jana Sangh 117
Japan 48, 107
Jayal, Niraja Gopal 164, 169
Jharkhand 145
Jinnah, Muhammad Ali 25, 35–36,
57–62, 64- 68, 70, 79–80,
83–84, 93–94, 130, 138–139
J&K. See Jammu
Judaism 147
Juggernaut 23–24
Junagadh 78, 83, 85, 87

Kali 143
Kapurthala 75
Karachi 73, 75, 82, 84, 98
Karnataka 113
Karunanidhi, Muthuvel 160
Kashmir 53, 75, 78–88, 90–91,
102, 107, 115–120, 124,
132–133, 135, 138, 144,
160, 175–179
Kaul, Brij Mohan (General) 129, 132
Kautilya 108

Kerala 5, 68, 109, 113, 132–136
Khalidi, Omar 90, 143
Khan, Liaquat Ali 62
Khilafat Movement 26
Khilnani, Sunil 8–9, 106
Khomeini, Ruhollah (Ayatollah)
18
Knesset 148
Kohima 122, 124
KPP (Krishak Praja Party) 58
Krishna 61, 88, 130, 132, 138, 150
Kumar, Nitish 159

Labour 61, 63, 76, 84
Lahore 59–62, 66, 89
Lamb, Alastair 80, 83, 116, 125
Lapierre, Dominique 64
Lenin, Vladimir 17
Liaquat Ali Khan 62
Likud 147–148
Lincoln, Abraham 9
Linlithgow, Lord 14, 47
Lloyd George, David 13
Lok Sabha 107–108, 132, 142, 148,
159, 167
LSE (London School of Econom-
ics) 52
Lucknow, Pact of 35

Macaulay, Thomas Babington 15
Madan, Triloki Nath 150
Madhya Pradesh 113
Madras 108, 113
Mahabharata 10, 51, 173–174
Maharashtra 99, 113
Mahatma Gandhi. See Gandhi,
Mohandas (Mahatma)
Maintenance of Internal Security
Act 170
Makarios III, Archbishop 18, 44
Malaya 63, 104, 123
Malaysia 104, 114
Malhotra, Jagmohan 175
Mali 115

Mandal, Bindeshwari Prasad
153–154, 157
Manekshaw, Sam (General) 84, 85
Manipur 10, 48, 120–121, 135, 179
Mann, Michael 111
Manu 108
Mao Zedong 17
Mapai 146
Marx, Karl 2, 17, 51
Mathai, M.O. 132
Mauritius 104
Maurya (dynasty) 10, 120
Maxwell, Neville 126
Mayawati 154–155
McMahon Line 125–129
Meghalaya 179
Mehta, Pratap Bhanu 8–9, 164, 169
Menon, Krishna 61, 132
Menon, Vappala Pangunni 68, 69,
75, 77, 82–84, 121
Messervy, Frank (General) 84
Michels, Robert 160
Mieville, Eric 71
Mizo 135
Mizoram 144, 179
Mohenjo-Daro 98
Mookerjee, Syama Prasad 117
Morley-Minto Reforms 16
Morocco 10
Motley, John Lothrop 51
Mountbatten 63–65, 67–70, 72,
75–77, 81–84, 88–89, 92,
101, 116
Mountbatten, Edwina 81
Mubarak, Hosni 178
Mughal (dynasty) 10, 12, 98, 120
Mullik, Bhola Nath 118, 122,
132–133
Muslim Conference (Kashmir) 78,
79, 85
Muslim League 35, 56–58, 60, 61,
64, 72, 78–80, 83, 89, 93,
95, 97, 137, 146
Mutiny, Indian 12, 17, 24, 27, 59, 63

Myanmar 176
Mysore, Maharajah of 83

Naga 121–124
Nagaland 124, 128, 144, 179
Naga National Council 121, 123
Nandy, Ashis 150
Nasser, Gamal Abdel 44
National Conference (Kashmir)
78–79, 85–86, 115–119
National Security Act 170
National Security Guards 143
Naxalite Movement 5, 145
Nehru, Jawaharlal 3, 7–10, 16,
31, 35, 42, 44, 47, 49–57,
59–63, 65, 67–73, 75,
80–82, 85–86, 89–91,
94–95, 97, 101–103, 105,
108–110, 113, 115–120,
122–124, 126–135, 138,
147, 152–154, 158–161,
170, 174–175, 181
Nehru, Motilal 94
Nepal 13, 121, 143
New York 103
Niebelunglied 10
Nigeria 115
Nixon, Richard 133
Nizam of Hyderabad (Osman Ali
Khan) 78–79
Non-Cooperation Movement
26–27, 29, 31–37, 50, 93, 94
Noorani, A.G. 90–91, 119
North-East India 10, 96, 120, 122,
128–129, 132, 135, 144, 179
North-West Frontier Province 13,
57, 69, 71–73, 82, 85,
115–116
NREGA 165–167

OBC. See Other Backward Classes
Odyssey 173
Orissa 47, 126
Oslo 178

Ostrogorsky, Moisey 160
Other Backward Classes 142, 154,
    157
Ottoman Empire 1, 24–26

Pakistan 41, 60, 66, 68–70, 73,
    75–86, 88–90, 93, 98, 115,
    137, 139–140, 142, 144,
    176–180
Palestine 76, 175
Palmerston, Lord 12
Pamban channel 173
Pant, Govind Ballabh 56
Paraguay 116
Patel, Vallabhbhai 47, 62, 65, 68, 77,
    81, 83, 86–88, 91, 108–109,
    121, 130–131, 133, 138,
    158, 169, 182
Pathans 71, 73, 82–83, 91
Patiala 74, 82
Pentateuch 18
Periyar. See Ramasamy, Erode
    Venkata (Periyar)
Peshawar 72
Philippines 115
Phizo, Angami Zapu 122
PLA 128–129
Poona 40–41, 50
Poonch 82
Praja Parishad 117
Presidential Rule 136, 161
Prevention of Insults to National
    Honour Act 170
Prevention of Terrorist Activities
    Act 170
Punjab 13, 26, 35, 58, 65–66, 69,
    70, 74–75, 81–83, 93, 109,
    143–144, 149

Qing court 125, 127
Queen Mary 134
Quit India Movement 44, 48
Quran 18

Radcliffe, Cyril 75–76, 82
Radha 138
Raghavan, Srinath 85, 126–127
Rajagopalachari, Chakravarti 131
Rajputs 97
Rama 22, 94, 152, 173
Ramachandra Guha 8–9, 106, 168
Ramarajya 22
Ramasamy, Erode Venkata (Periyar)
    172
Ramayana 24, 173
Ram, Jagjivan 139
Rangoon 47, 120, 126
Rao, P.V. Narasimha 149, 159
Rau, Benegal Narsing 75, 107–108
Ravana 22, 173
Rawalpindi 118
RAW (Research and Analysis Wing)
    143
Red Shirts 71–73, 85
Renan, Ernest 89
Roberts, Andrew 64
Roosevelt, Franklin Delano 9
Round Table Conferences 36, 45,
    93
Roy, Arundhati 177
RSS 18, 147–149, 181
Ruskin, John 51
Russia 1, 48, 125, 178

Sachar Commission 141, 142
Sadat, Anwar 178
Sadiq, Ghulam Mohammad
    118–119
Saigon 105
Salisbury, Lord 13
Sarkar, Sumit 74
Savarkar, Vinayak Damodar 89,
    143, 151
Scheduled Castes' Federation 138
Scott, James 120
Sen, Amartya 8–9, 140, 150, 176
Sèvres, Treaty of 26
Shastri, Lal Bahadur 128

Shevetbindu Rameshwar 23
Shillong 121, 124
Sikh insurgency 149
Sikkim 179
Sima Qian 174
Simla 68, 124–126
Sindh 57
Singapore 47–48, 114
Singh, Manmohan 7–8, 159
Sita 173
South Africa 2, 16, 18, 22–23, 28, 32, 51–52
Soviet Union 63
Special Protection Group 143
Sri Lanka 91, 99, 104, 173
Srinagar 82–83, 87, 91, 116–117, 124, 128
Stephens, Ian 82–84
Sudan 114
Suhrawardy, Huseyn Shaheed 70
Sukarno 44
Sundarlal Report 91
Supreme Court of India 104, 119, 155, 161, 173
Surabaya 105
Switzerland 78, 89, 115

Taiwan 131
Talbott, Strobe 178
Tamilnadu 160
Tanjore 103
Tel Aviv 178
Telugu 113
Terrorism and Disruptive Activities Act 170
Thagla Ridge 129
Tibet 124, 126, 135, 175
Tibetan rebels 126
Tidrick 2, 18–19
Tidrick, Kathryn 2, 18

Tokyo 48
Tolstoy, Leo 22, 51
Trautmann, Thomas 174
Trimurti 173, 179
Tripura 120–121, 135

Unionist Party (Punjab) 58
Unity of India, The 10, 52, 61, 81
Unlawful Activities Amendment Act 170
Unlawful Activities Prevention Act 170
U Nu 122, 141
Upanishads 128, 133
Urdu 58
US 129, 141, 144, 179

Vajpeyi, Ananya 144
Valley (of Kashmir) 82, 84–86, 90, 115–117, 119, 175, 179
Vanaik, Achin 140, 149, 165, 172
Vande Mataram 99
Verma, Arvind 170
Vietnam 91–92, 123
Vishnu 99

Washington, George 9
Wavell, Archibald 29, 61–62
Weber, Max 102
Western Sahara 115
Westminster 95, 107
Widgery, Lord 75
Wikileaks 141
Witzel, Michael 174
Wood, Charles 12

Youlou, Abbé Fulbert 18

Zhou Enlai 119, 126, 174
Zulu rebellion of 1906 28

Index of Authorities

Adhikari, Gangadhar 90
Ahmad, Aijaz 74
Ahmed, Ishtiaq 75
Ahsan, Aitzaz 98
Akbar Khan 82
Alam, Javeed 128, 155, 156
Ali, Tariq 85
Austin, Granville 108

Balachandran, G. 98, 152
Bannerjee, Mukulika 73
Bardhan, Pranab 162–163
Barnes, John 46
Baruah, Sanjib 121, 144
Basu, Kaushik 152
Baxi, Upendra 161
Bayly, Christopher 13
Behera, Navnita Chadha 178
Béteille, Andre 37, 160
Bhargava, Rajeev 140
Bose, Sugata 43
Bose, Sumantra 177
Brass, Paul 134, 170
Brown, Judith 16, 43, 49, 110

Campbell-Johnson, Alan 64, 69, 101
Chakrabarty, Bidyut 71
Chatterji, Joya 71
Chaudhuri, Nirad 99, 151
Clarke, Peter 14

Cohen, Stephen 12, 77, 171
Collins, Larry 64
Conboy, Kenneth 126
Connell, John 89
Copland, Ian 68, 80
Crocker, Walter 130–131

Das, Durga 86, 101
Desai, Meghnad 8–9, 65, 95, 174
Desai, Radhika 151–152
Dua, Bhagwan 134
Dutta, Puja 166

Embree, Ainslie 11

Fischer, Louis 51
Fravel, M. Taylor 127
French, Patrick 135, 160

Galanter, Marc 156
Gandhi, Rajmohan 18
Gopal, Sarvepalli 124, 130
Gordon, Leonard 71
Guha, Ramachandra 8–9, 106, 168, 169
Gupta, Dipankar 155

Harper, Tim 13
Hasan, Mushirul 36, 74, 153
Hasan, Zoya 107, 165

Hoffman, Steven 129

Jaffrelot, Christophe 154
Jalal, Ayesha 60, 65
Jeffrey, Robin 92
Jha, Prem Shankar 85

Keera, Reetika 166
Khalidi, Omar 90, 143
Khilnani, Sunil 8–9, 106
Korbel, Joseph 82
Krishna, B. 88, 130
Kudaisya, Gyanesh 103

Lapierre, Dominique 64
Lasuh, W. 123
Lelyveld, Joseph 18
Low, D.A. 45–46, 80, 136
Luce, Edward 156, 162–163

Mahadevan, T.K. 52
Mahajan, Sucheta 88
Mansergh, Nicholas 14
Marquand, David 76
Mathai, M.O. 132
Maxwell, Neville 126–129
Mehta, Pratap Bhanu 8–9, 164, 169
Mendelsohn, Oliver 156
Menon, Krishna 61, 132
Middlemas, Kenneth 46
Misra, B.B. 11, 97
Morrison, James 126
Mosley, Leonard 68, 89
Mullik, B.N. 118, 122, 132–133
Murgai, Rinku 166

Nibedon, Nirmal 122
Noorani, A.G. 90, 91, 119

Omissi, David 13

Prasad, Bimal 56
Puri, Balraj 120
Pyarelal 40, 72

Raghavan, Srinath 85, 126–127
Ravallion, Martin 166
Raychaudhuri, Tapan 15
Reeves, Peter 110
Roberts, Andrew 64
Roy, Asim 67
Rubin, Alfred 125

Sarkar, Sumit 74
Sarkar, Tanika 99
Schofield, Victoria 82, 88, 175
Sen, Amartya 8–9, 140, 150, 176
Singh, Hira Lal 12
Sridharan, E. 107
Stephens, Ian 82–84
Subrahmanyam, Sanjay 97, 152

Talbot, Ian 77, 93
Tomlinson, B.R. 46
Trautmann, Thomas 174

Vajpeyi, Ananya 144, 145
Vanaik, Achin 140, 149, 165, 172
Van der Walle, Dominique 166
Venkatachar, C.S. 47
Verma, Arvind 170
Vicziany, Marika 156

Wavell, Archibald 29, 61–62
Witzel, Michael 174
Wolpert, Stanley 34, 56, 130

Yadav, Yogendra 164
Yong, Tan Tai 58, 74, 103

Zachariah, Benjamin 90
Ziegler, Philip 81